THE STORY OF MY TITS

THE STORY OF MY TITS

Jennifer Hayden

Top Shelf Productions

I lay this book at the feet of the Goddess.

I also dedicate it to Mary, whose absence will always bring tears.

And to my husband, who has the kind of loyalty and devotion they just don't make anymore.

Story of My Tits © & ™ 2015 Jennifer Hayden

Published by
Top Shelf Productions
PO Box 1282
Marietta, GA 30061-1282
USA

Editor-in-Chief: Chris Staros

Edited by Chris Staros and Leigh Walton.
Cover design by Briar Levit, Michelle Leigh, and Chris Ross.

Visit our online catalog at www.topshelfcomix.com.

Printed in Korea.

ISBN 978-1-60309-054-4

18   17   16   15   5   4   3   2   1

This story is a dramatic comedy sewn together from real events and real emotions. Names, places, dates, dialogue, and even people have been changed to protect the integrity of the tale.

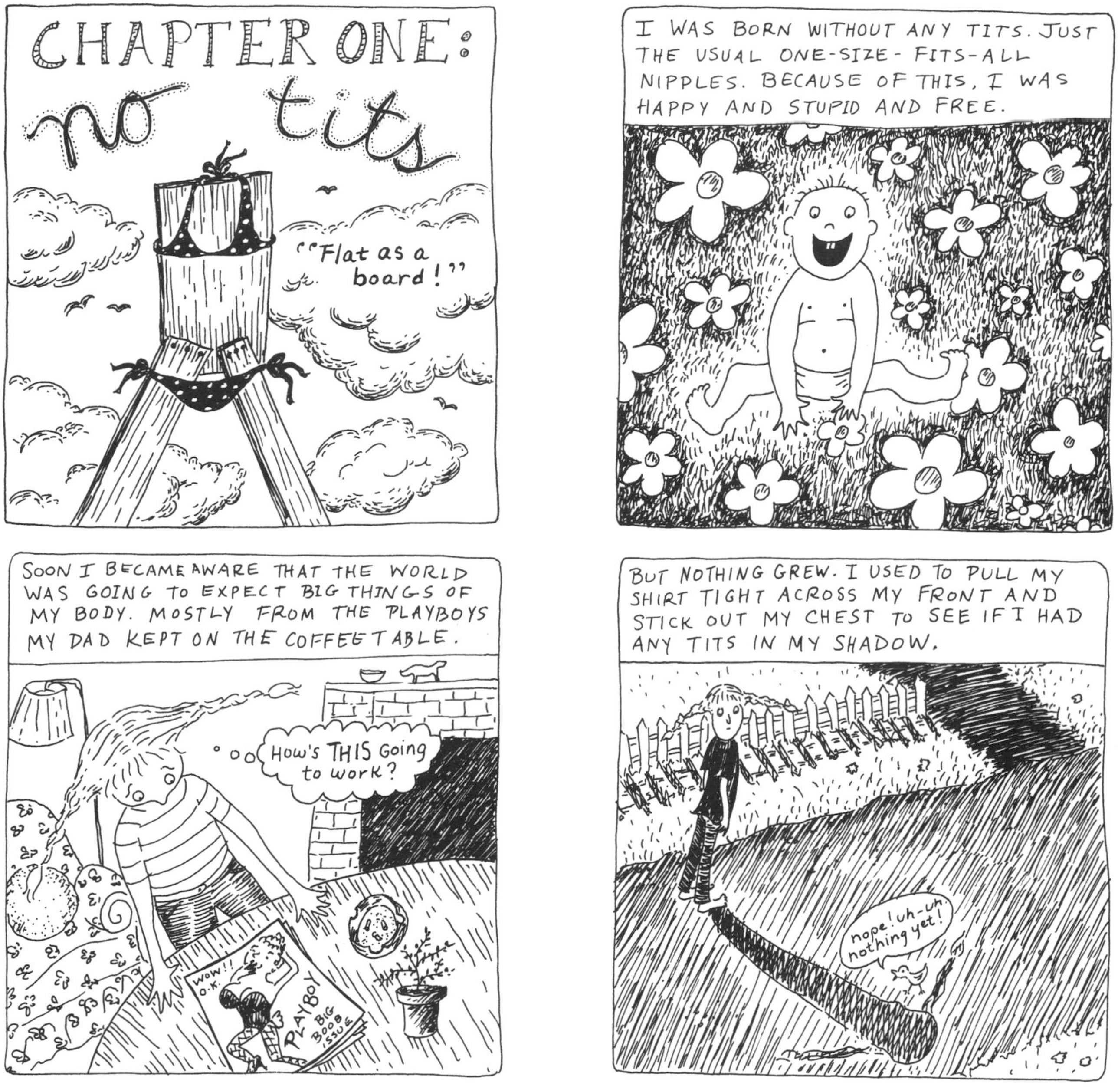
CHAPTER ONE:
no tits
"Flat as a board!"
I WAS BORN WITHOUT ANY TITS. JUST THE USUAL ONE-SIZE-FITS-ALL NIPPLES. BECAUSE OF THIS, I WAS HAPPY AND STUPID AND FREE.
SOON I BECAME AWARE THAT THE WORLD WAS GOING TO EXPECT BIG THINGS OF MY BODY. MOSTLY FROM THE PLAYBOYS MY DAD KEPT ON THE COFFEE TABLE.
How's THIS Going to work?
WOW!! O.K.
PLAYBOY
BIG BOOB ISSUE
BUT NOTHING GREW. I USED TO PULL MY SHIRT TIGHT ACROSS MY FRONT AND STICK OUT MY CHEST TO SEE IF I HAD ANY TITS IN MY SHADOW.
nope! uh-uh nothing yet!

MY BEST FRIEND MARGIE AND I USED TO STUFF OUR BIKINIS WITH ROCKS SO WE'D LOOK STACKED.

BUT NOTHING GREW.

I THOUGHT IF I JUST SHOWED A LITTLE FAITH.

SHE TALKED TO MY FATHER ABOUT IT.

MY FATHER SAID HE DIDN'T SEE WHY I NEEDED A BRA WHEN I DIDN'T HAVE ANYTHING GROWING UP THERE.

I WAS MORTIFIED.

NOW I WANTED TITS MORE THAN ANYTHING IN THE WORLD. I THOUGHT THEY WERE THE ANSWER TO ALL MY PROBLEMS.

I THOUGHT I'D BE MORE LIKE MY MOM IF I HAD TITS.

9

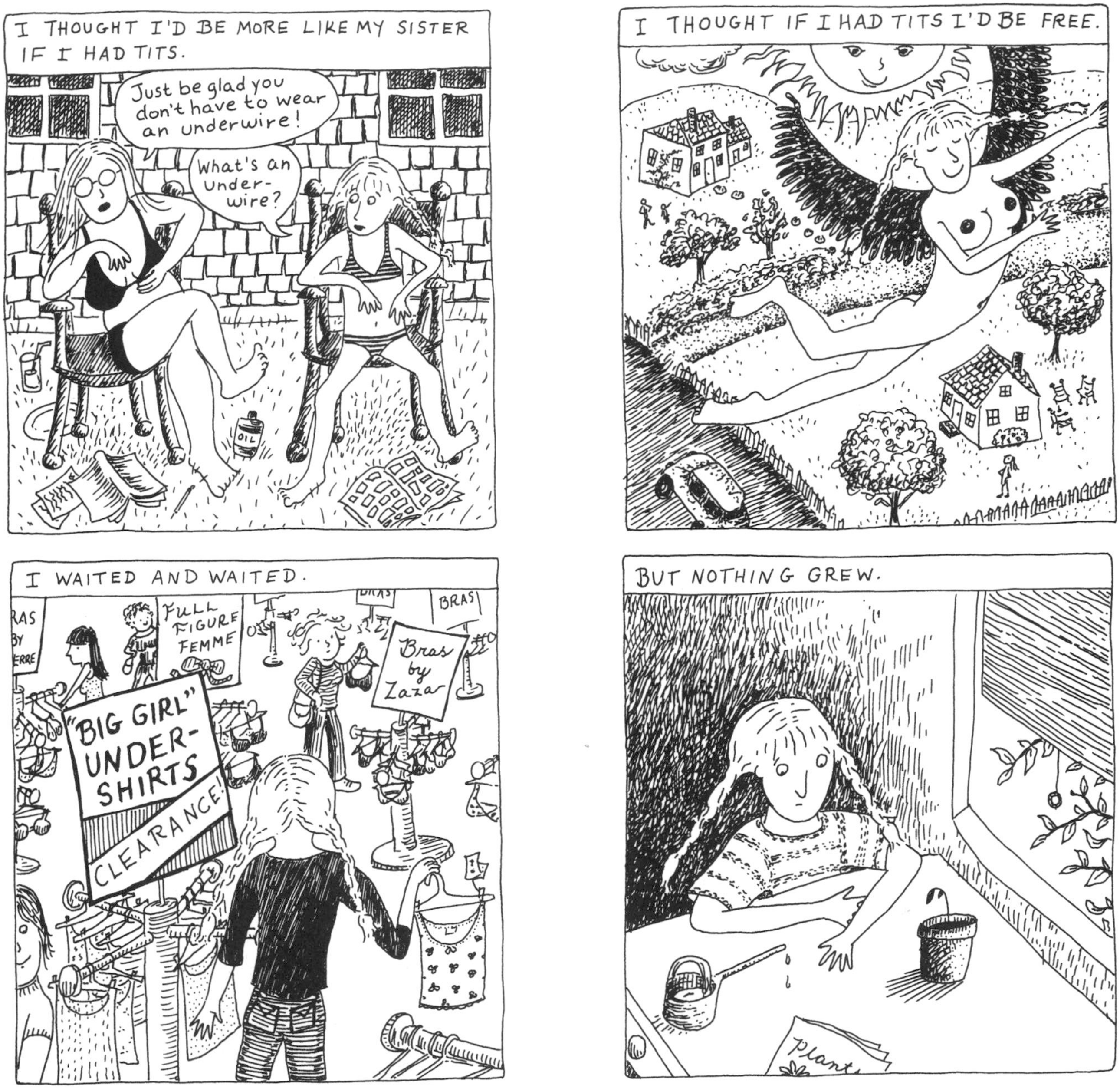
I THOUGHT I'D BE MORE LIKE MY SISTER IF I HAD TITS.
Just be glad you don't have to wear an underwire!
What's an under-wire?
OIL
I THOUGHT IF I HAD TITS I'D BE FREE.
I WAITED AND WAITED.
FULL FIGURE FEMME
BRAS
Bras by Zaza
"BIG GIRL" UNDER-SHIRTS
CLEARANCE!
BUT NOTHING GREW.

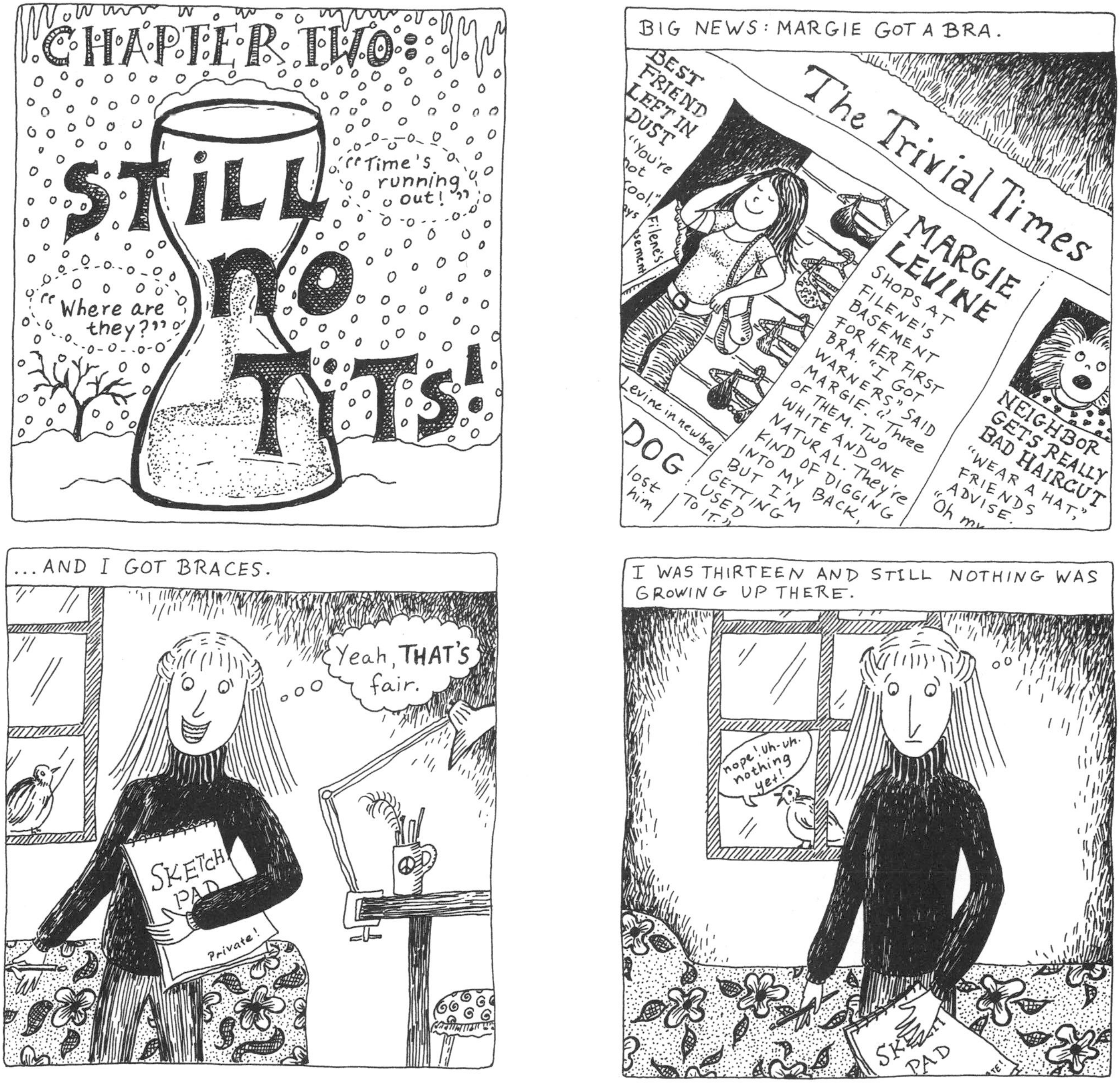
CHAPTER TWO:
STILL NO TITS!
"Time's running out!"
"Where are they?"
BIG NEWS: MARGIE GOT A BRA.
The Trivial Times
BEST FRIEND LEFT IN DUST
"You're
Filene's
Levine in new bra
MARGIE LEVINE
SHOPS AT FILENE'S BASEMENT FOR HER FIRST BRA. "I GOT WARNERS," SAID MARGIE. "Three OF THEM. TWO WHITE AND ONE NATURAL. They're KIND OF DIGGING INTO MY BACK, BUT I'M GETTING USED TO IT."
NEIGHBOR GETS REALLY BAD HAIRCUT
"WEAR A HAT," FRIENDS ADVISE.
DOG
lost him
...AND I GOT BRACES.
Yeah, THAT'S fair.
SKETCH PAD
Private!
I WAS THIRTEEN AND STILL NOTHING WAS GROWING UP THERE.
nope! uh-uh. nothing yet!

SO I WAS TRYING A FEW NEW THINGS.

#1 - New hair-style: older! Also kind of artsy, which is becoming my look.

#2 - WRITING POETRY. MOSTLY ABOUT BOYS I DON'T KNOW.

#3 - MODERN DANCE. IT ALLOWS ME TO EXPRESS MY FEELINGS AND IS ALSO A GOOD EXCUSE TO WEAR A LEOTARD ON NORMAL DAYS.

WHICH MIGHT HAVE BEEN SEXY, IF THERE HAD BEEN ANYTHING UNDER IT.

BUT THERE WASN'T.

DID I MENTION SHE WAS MY BEST FRIEND?

I ASKED MY BEST FRIEND NORAH IF SHE THOUGHT GUYS WERE ONLY INTERESTED IN TITS.

AND EVEN IF MY CHEST REFUSED TO COOPERATE, THERE WERE OTHER WAYS TO LOOK OLDER.

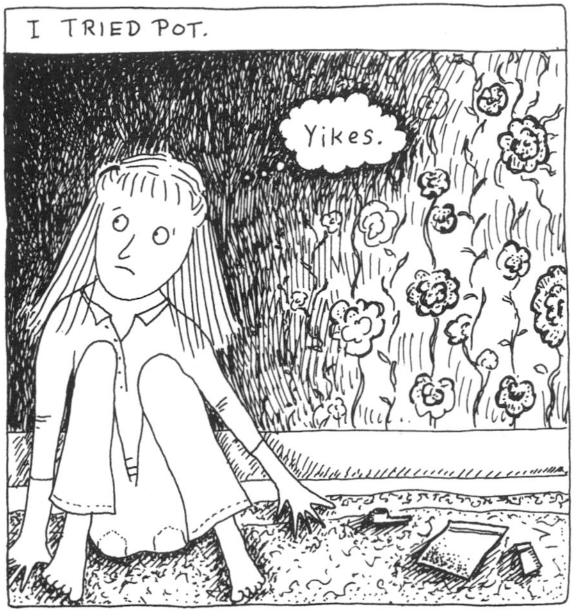
I TRIED POT.
Yikes.

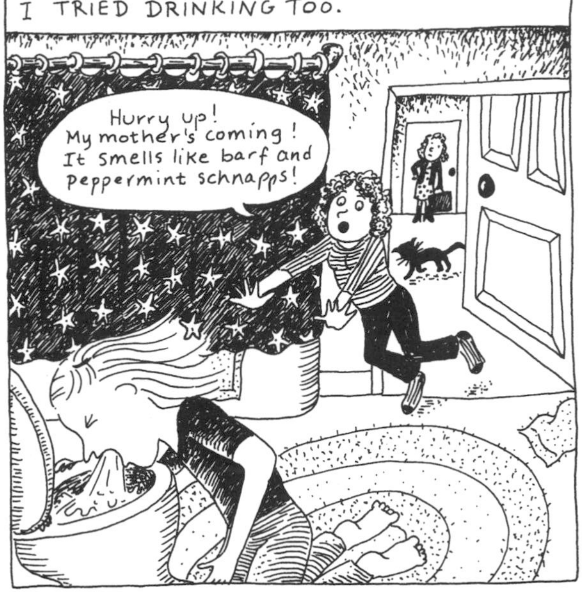
I TRIED DRINKING TOO.
Hurry up! My mother's coming! It smells like barf and peppermint schnapps!

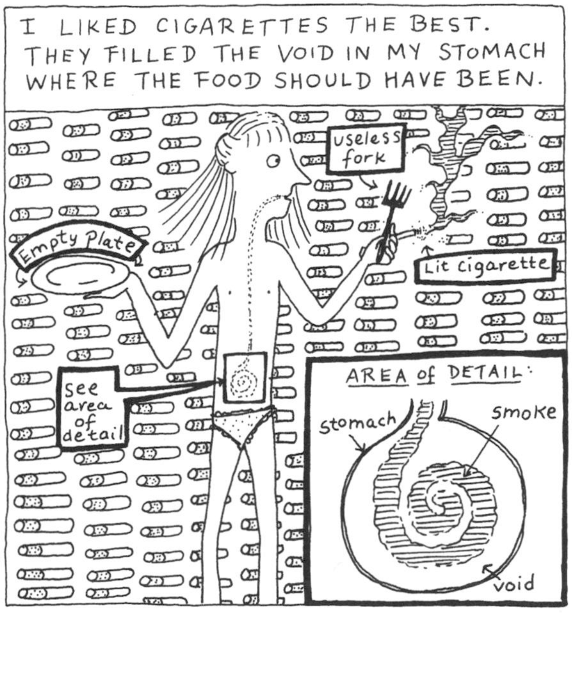
I LIKED CIGARETTES THE BEST. THEY FILLED THE VOID IN MY STOMACH WHERE THE FOOD SHOULD HAVE BEEN.
useless fork
Empty Plate
Lit cigarette
See area of detail
AREA of DETAIL:
stomach
smoke
void

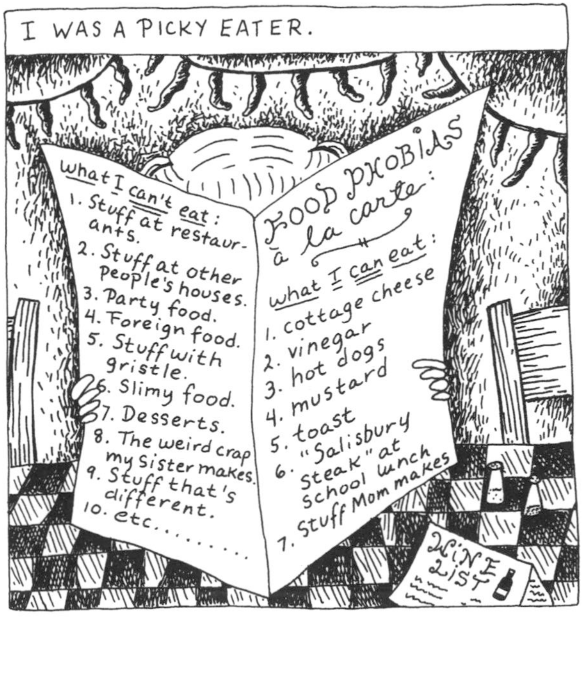
I WAS A PICKY EATER.
what I can't eat:
1. Stuff at restaurants.
2. Stuff at other People's houses.
3. Party food.
4. Foreign food.
5. Stuff with gristle.
6. Slimy food.
7. Desserts.
8. The weird crap my sister makes.
9. Stuff that's different.
10. etc........
FOOD PHOBIAS à la carte:
what I can eat:
1. cottage cheese
2. vinegar
3. hot dogs
4. mustard
5. toast
6. "Salisbury Steak" at school lunch
7. Stuff Mom makes
WINE LIST

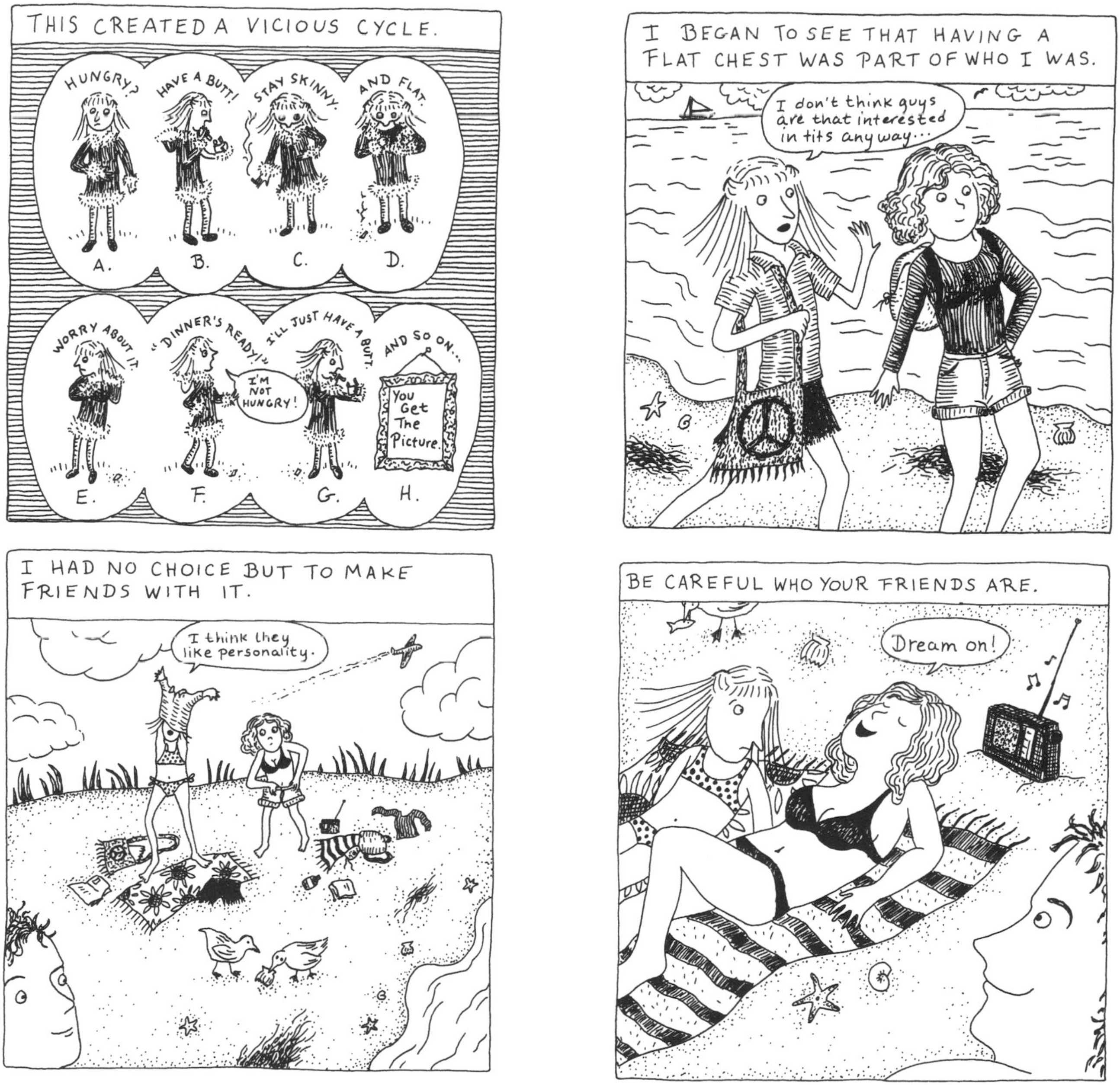
THIS CREATED A VICIOUS CYCLE.
HUNGRY?
HAVE A BUTT!
STAY SKINNY.
AND FLAT.
A.
B.
C.
D.
WORRY ABOUT IT.
"DINNER'S READY!"
I'M NOT HUNGRY!
I'LL JUST HAVE A BUTT.
AND SO ON...
You Get The Picture.
E.
F.
G.
H.
I BEGAN TO SEE THAT HAVING A FLAT CHEST WAS PART OF WHO I WAS.
I don't think guys are that interested in tits anyway...
I HAD NO CHOICE BUT TO MAKE FRIENDS WITH IT.
I think they like personality.
BE CAREFUL WHO YOUR FRIENDS ARE.
Dream on!

CHAPTER THREE:

?What, Tits?

"Really?" "You sure?"

THEN — SOMETHING STARTED TO GROW.

GREAT. STILL NO TITS, BUT I'VE GOT THE BIGGEST NIPPLES IN THE WORLD.

ONE NIGHT I GOT DRESSED UP AND WENT OVER TO MY FRIEND KATHERINE'S BEFORE THE DANCE.

You can't wear that! I can totally see your nipples through that dress! You need a bra!

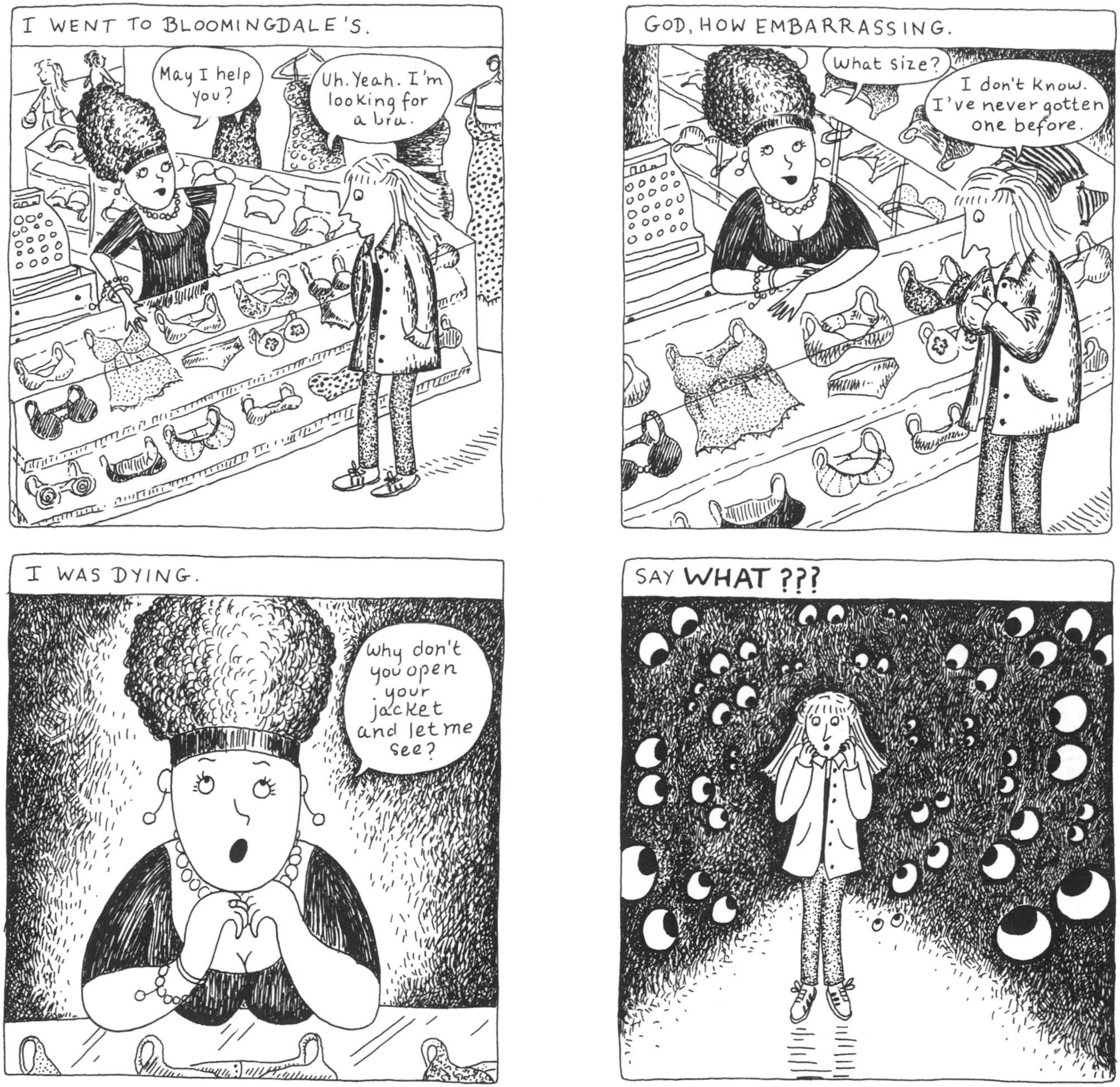
I WENT TO BLOOMINGDALE'S.
May I help you?
Uh. Yeah. I'm looking for a bra.
GOD, HOW EMBARRASSING.
What size?
I don't know. I've never gotten one before.
I WAS DYING.
Why don't you open your jacket and let me see?
SAY **WHAT ???**

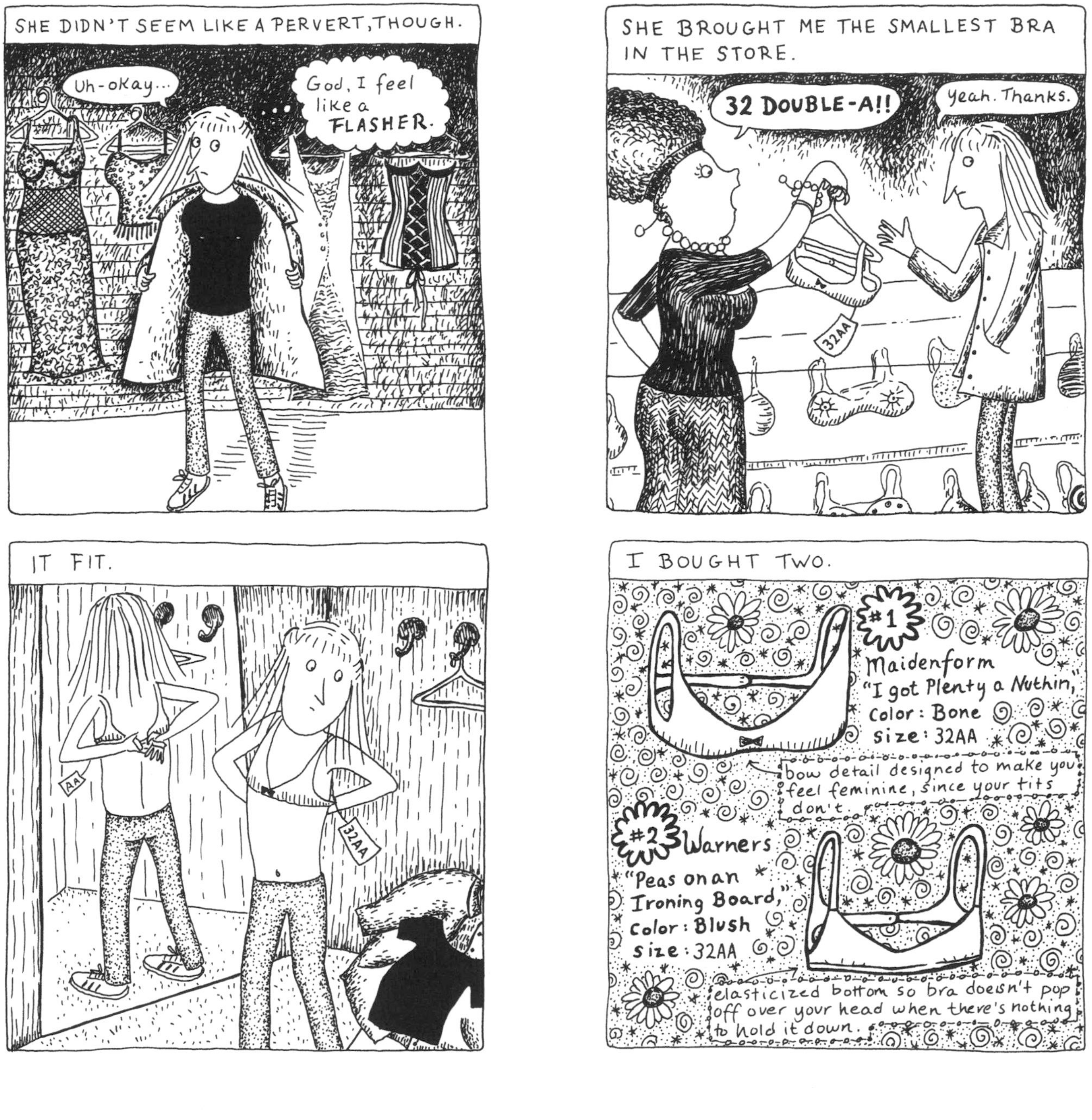
SHE DIDN'T SEEM LIKE A PERVERT, THOUGH.
Uh-okay...
God, I feel like a FLASHER.
SHE BROUGHT ME THE SMALLEST BRA IN THE STORE.
32 DOUBLE-A!!
Yeah. Thanks.
32AA
IT FIT.
AA
32AA
I BOUGHT TWO.
#1
Maidenform
"I got Plenty a Nuthin"
Color: Bone
size: 32AA
bow detail designed to make you feel feminine, since your tits don't.
#2
Warners
"Peas on an Ironing Board,"
Color: Blush
size: 32AA
elasticized bottom so bra doesn't pop off over your head when there's nothing to hold it down.

SOMEHOW, IT WASN'T THE VICTORY I HAD IMAGINED.

I HAD A FEELING MY LIFE HAD JUST GOTTEN MORE COMPLICATED.

IT WASN'T GOING TO BE THE WAY IT WAS WHEN I WAS TEN YEARS OLD ANYMORE...

NOW IT WAS A TOTAL DRAG.

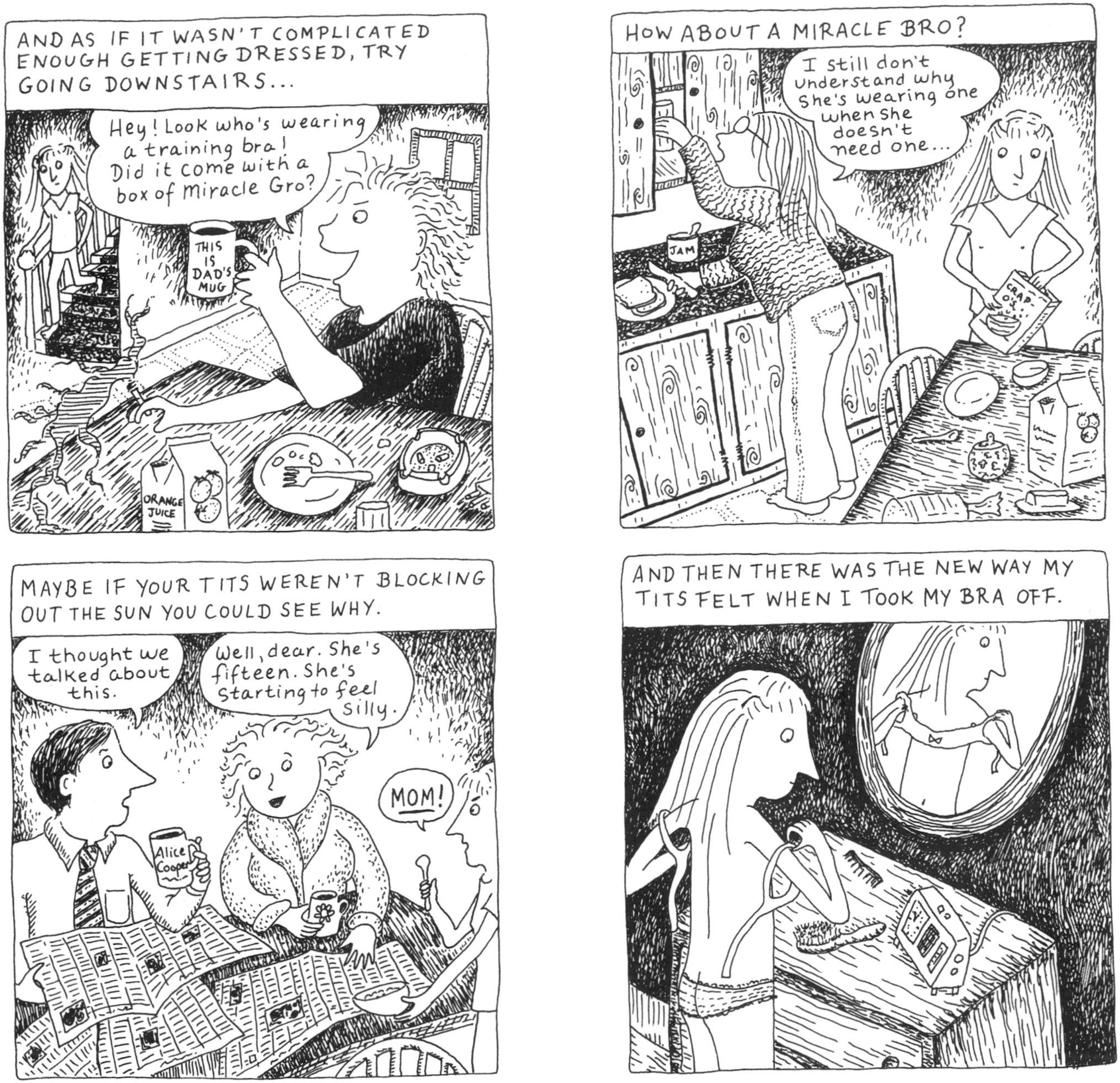
AND AS IF IT WASN'T COMPLICATED ENOUGH GETTING DRESSED, TRY GOING DOWNSTAIRS...
Hey! Look who's wearing a training bra! Did it come with a box of Miracle Gro?
THIS IS DAD'S MUG
ORANGE JUICE
HOW ABOUT A MIRACLE BRO?
I still don't understand why she's wearing one when she doesn't need one...
JAM
CRAP-O's
MAYBE IF YOUR TITS WEREN'T BLOCKING OUT THE SUN YOU COULD SEE WHY.
I thought we talked about this.
Well, dear. She's fifteen. She's starting to feel silly.
MOM!
Alice Cooper
AND THEN THERE WAS THE NEW WAY MY TITS FELT WHEN I TOOK MY BRA OFF.

NOW THEY FELT NAKED.

AND SENSITIVE.

ALMOST LIKE THEY WERE TRANSMITTING SOME SORT OF MESSAGE.

AND THE MESSAGE WAS:

HEY, BOYS!

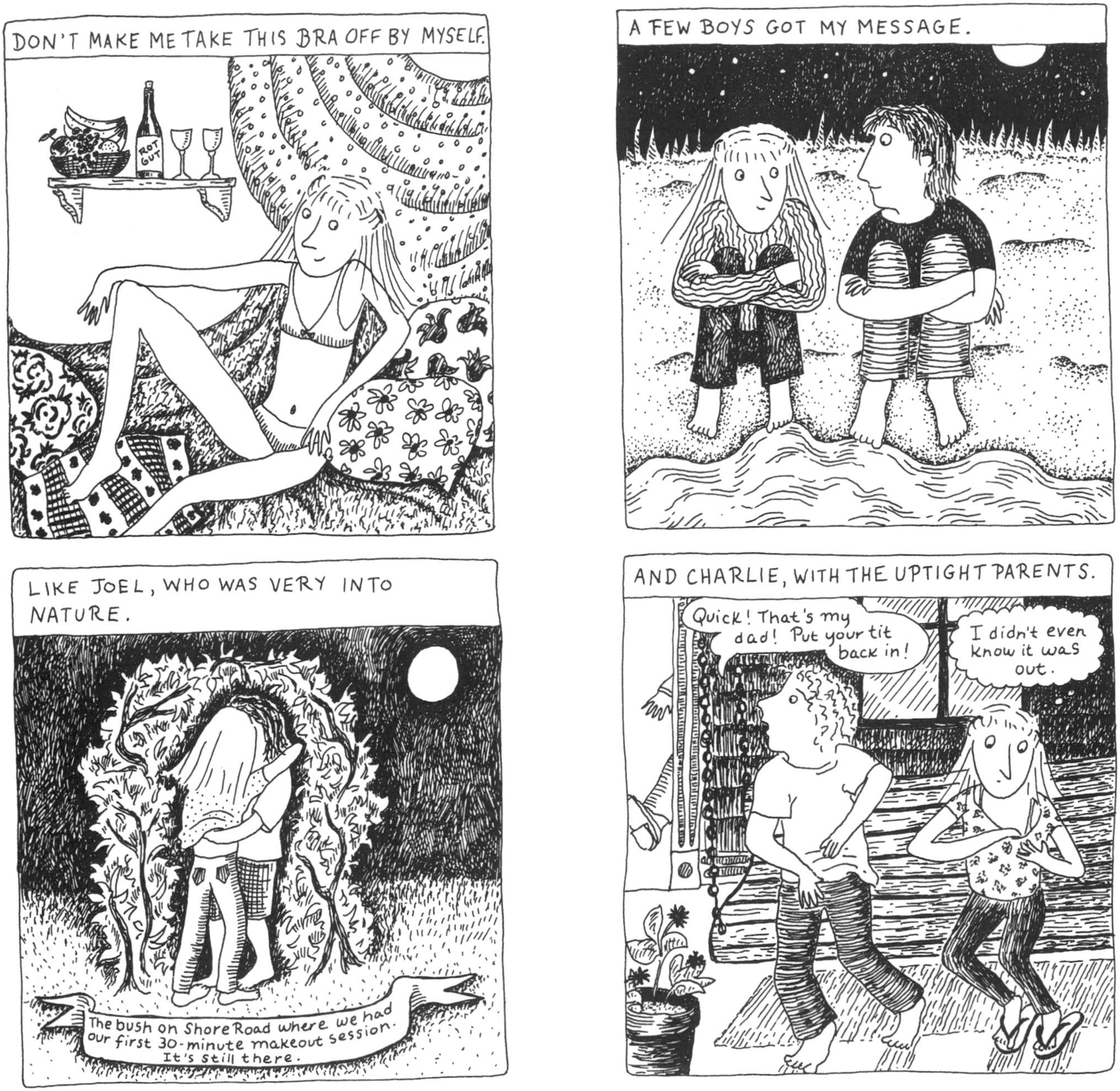
DON'T MAKE ME TAKE THIS BRA OFF BY MYSELF.
ROT GUT
A FEW BOYS GOT MY MESSAGE.
LIKE JOEL, WHO WAS VERY INTO NATURE.
The bush on Shore Road where we had our first 30-minute makeout session. It's still there.
AND CHARLIE, WITH THE UPTIGHT PARENTS.
Quick! That's my dad! Put your tit back in!
I didn't even know it was out.

AND THE MOTORCYCLE GUY IN WELLFLEET.

AND ADAM THE WRESTLER.

Do you think we're ready?

Ready for what?

I WAS A LITTLE FUZZY ABOUT WHAT WAS SUPPOSED TO HAPPEN ONCE THE BRA CAME OFF.

BUT I KNEW IT WOULD BE GOOD.

MY SISTER'S BOYFRIEND SAID: "COLLEGE IS JUST HIGH SCHOOL WITH ASHTRAYS."

Would you get off me, Yanni? You're drunk.

BUT I WOULD HAVE DESCRIBED IT DIFFERENTLY.

VERY DIFFERENTLY.

FOR ME, IT WASN'T ABOUT THE ASHTRAYS.

CONDOMS ↓

IT WAS ABOUT FEELING ACCEPTED NO MATTER WHAT MY TITS LOOKED LIKE.

Le freak! C'est chic!

IT WAS ABOUT NEW HAIRSTYLES AND NEW FRIENDS EVERY NIGHT.

Voulez-vous couchez avec moi, ce soir?

AND DURING THE DAY, IT WAS ABOUT GETTING AN EDUCATION.

Look. You just go to the infirmary and tell them you want an OBGYN appointment. Then you tell the doctor you want to get fitted for a diaphragm. I'll show you how to put it in.

freshman English
GREEK ART
STRUNK & WHITE
MUSIC THEORY
THE BIG BOOK OF ART HISTORY STUFF
HISTORICA
POLIT
ENCE
ELECTRIC TYPEWRITER C. 1979 A.D.

25

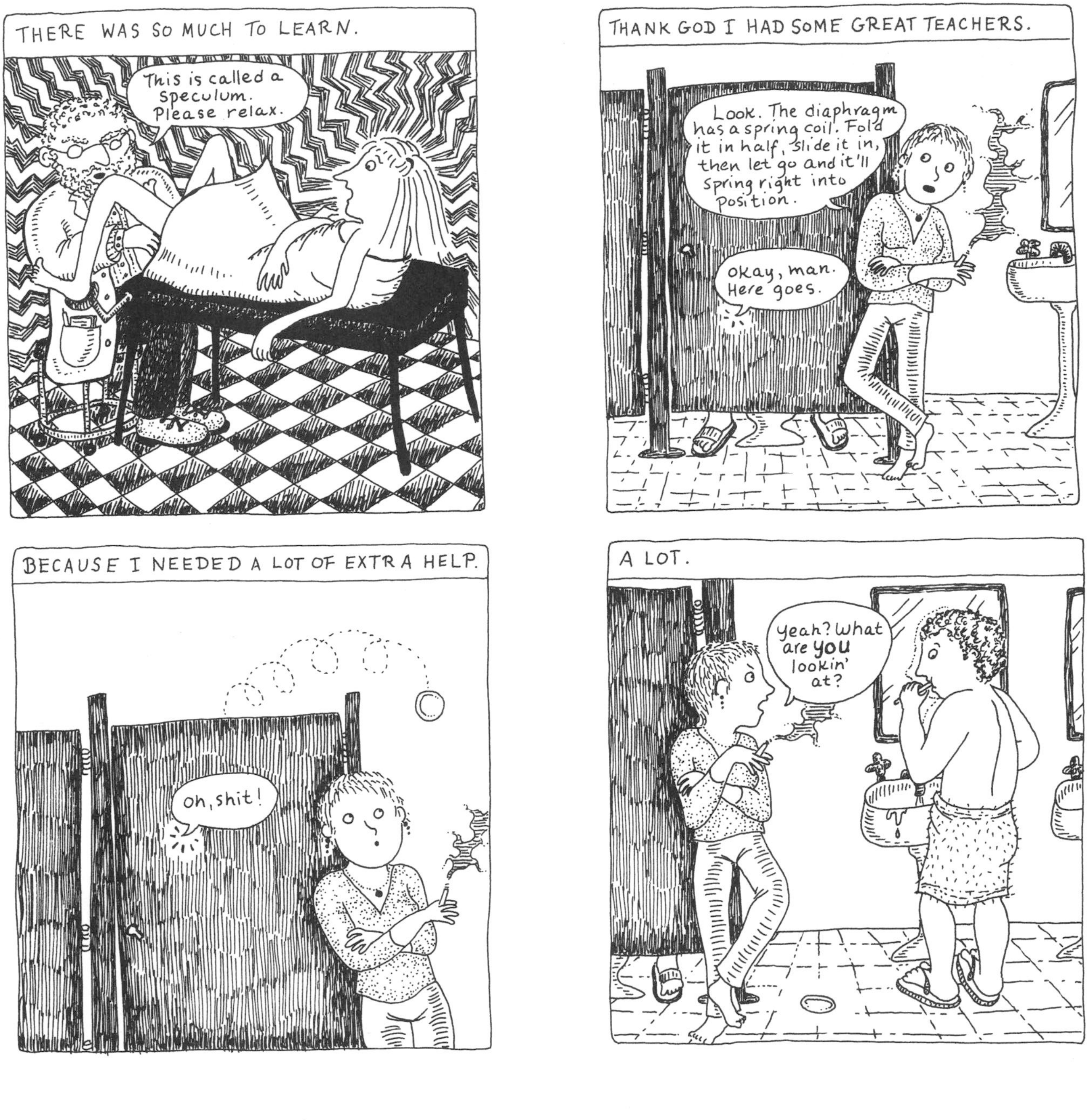
THERE WAS SO MUCH TO LEARN.
This is called a speculum. Please relax.
THANK GOD I HAD SOME GREAT TEACHERS.
Look. The diaphragm has a spring coil. Fold it in half, slide it in, then let go and it'll spring right into position.
okay, man. Here goes.
BECAUSE I NEEDED A LOT OF EXTRA HELP.
oh, shit!
A LOT.
Yeah? What are YOU lookin' at?

REALLY.

Uh...can I have that back?

EVENTUALLY, MY SKILLS IMPROVED.

I got it.

AND SO DID MY TITS.

If I told you you had a good body, would you hold it against me?

God, Parker, you're so desperate!

THEY WERE SMALL, BUT THEY HAD BIG ADMIRERS.

27

THERE WAS A WIDE RANGE OF TASTES OUT THERE, I DISCOVERED.

I touched them! I touched them!

I have Boob Power?

AND I MIGHT BE ONE OF THEM.

You have no idea how beautiful you are. I want you to remember that when you were twenty you had an absolutely perfect body.

huh?

SMALL TITS AND ALL.

What do you mean?*

Come on. Endless arms and legs, flat stomach, perfect little tits.

* English translation: tell me more about how great I look.

IT WAS FLATTERING, BUT WEIRD.

We don't have to do anything if you don't want to...

I don't want to.

28

AND MY TITS BASKED IN THE SUN OF THIS NEW APPRECIATION.

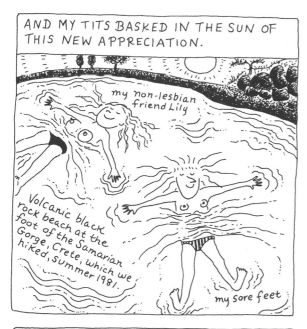

WELL, MOST OF THE TIME.

* Not the part of my body he was looking at.

AND THEN LOVE CAME DOWN AND HIT ME ON THE HEAD.

FUNNY, NOW THAT I HAD TITS, I FOUND OUT THAT BOYS LIKED PERSONALITY...

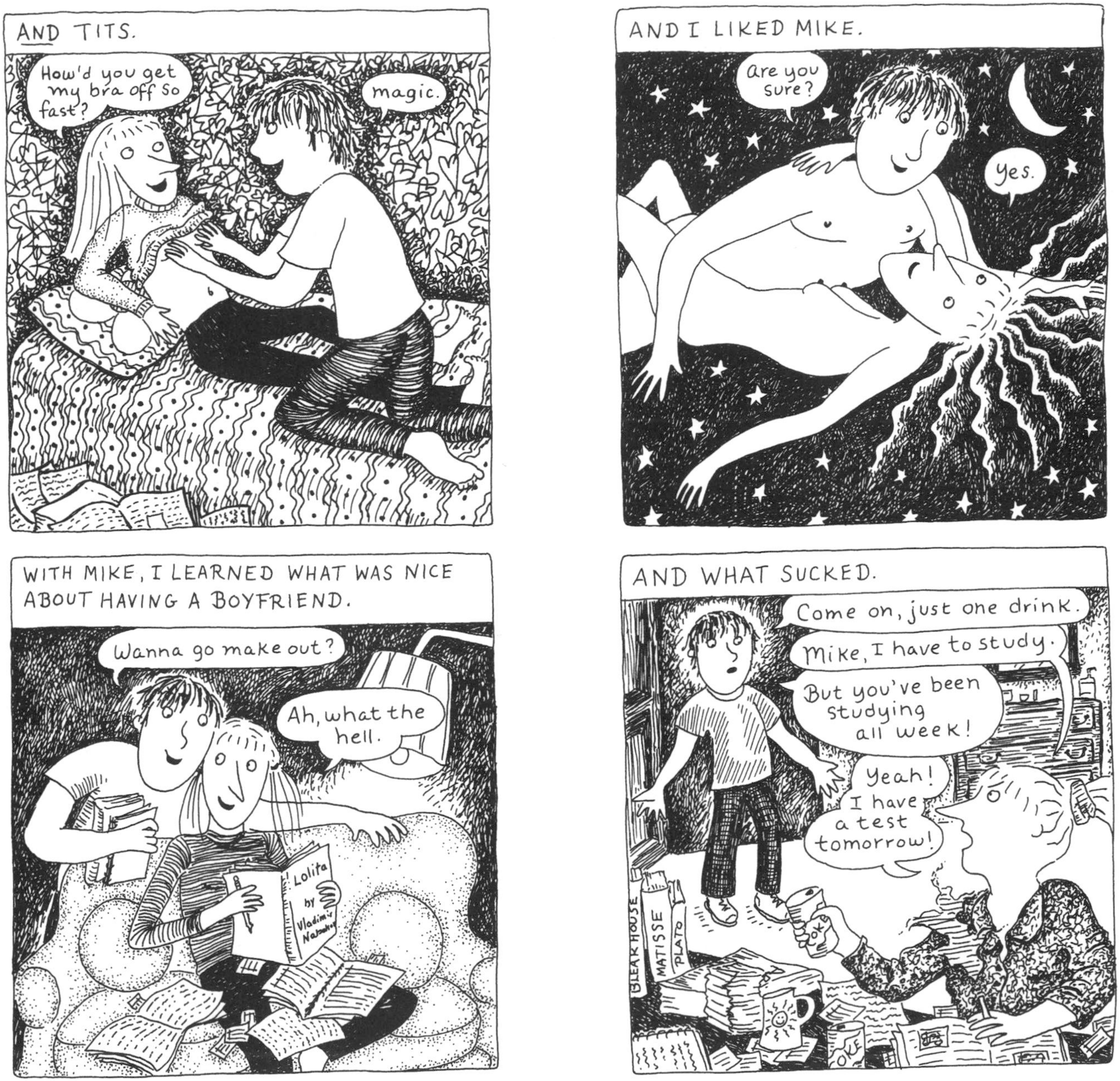
AND TITS.
How'd you get my bra off so fast?
magic.
AND I LIKED MIKE.
Are you sure?
Yes.
WITH MIKE, I LEARNED WHAT WAS NICE ABOUT HAVING A BOYFRIEND.
Wanna go make out?
Ah, what the hell.
Lolita by Vladimir
AND WHAT SUCKED.
Come on, just one drink.
Mike, I have to study.
But you've been studying all week!
Yeah! I have a test tomorrow!
BLEAK HOUSE
MATISSE
PLATO

I DECIDED TO GO WHERE I WOULD BE APPRECIATED.

I MEAN, HOW HARD COULD IT BE?

31

TOO HARD.

MUCH EASIER, I THOUGHT, TO GO OUT WITH HAL, WHO WAS DEEPLY ENMESHED IN A SMOLDERING LOVE TRIANGLE.

HE WAS A HEAD CASE.

BUT THAT ONLY MADE ME LOVE HIM MORE.

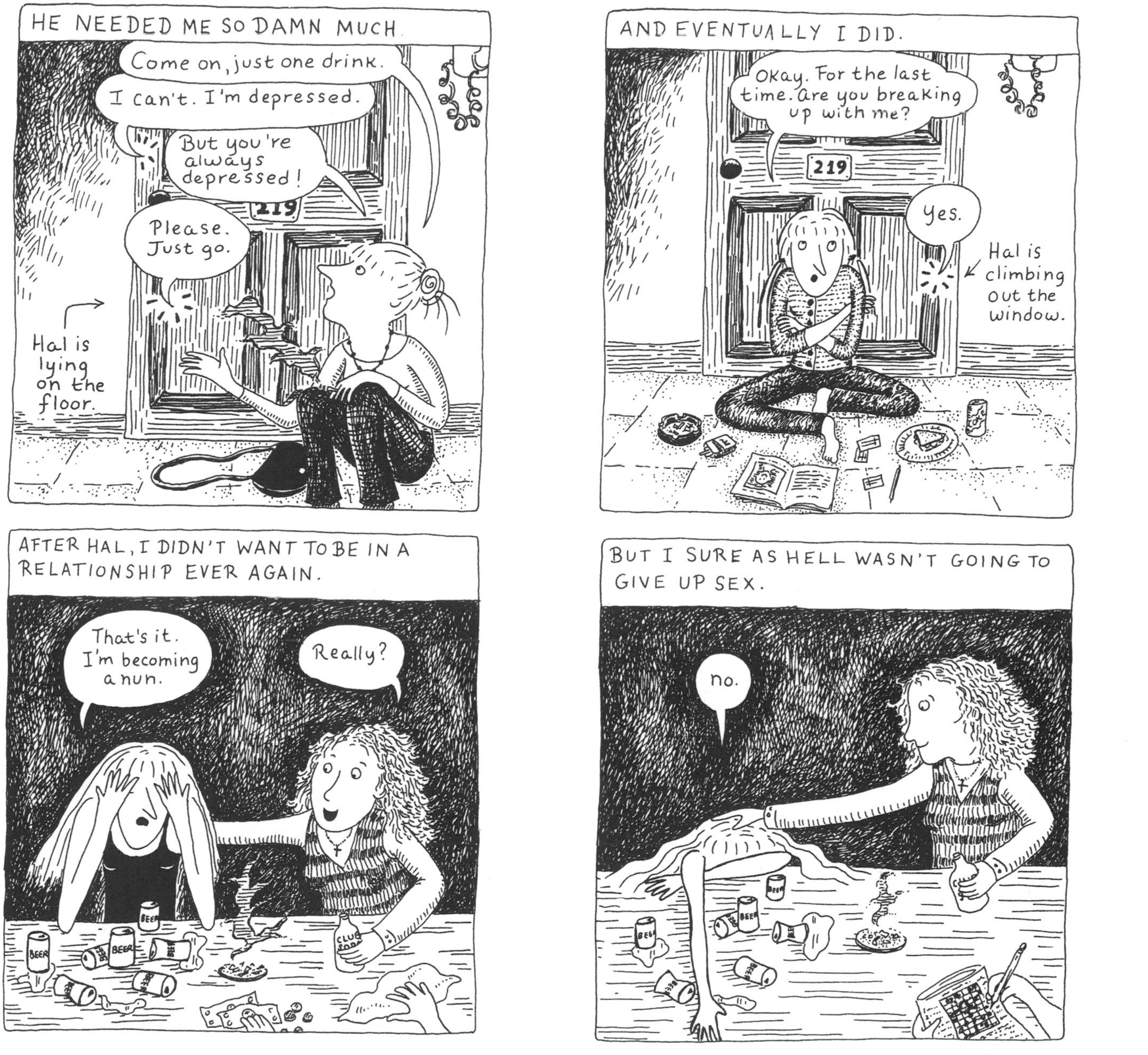
HE NEEDED ME SO DAMN MUCH.
Come on, just one drink.
I can't. I'm depressed.
But you're always depressed!
Please. Just go.
Hal is lying on the floor.
AND EVENTUALLY I DID.
Okay. For the last time. Are you breaking up with me?
Yes.
Hal is climbing out the window.
AFTER HAL, I DIDN'T WANT TO BE IN A RELATIONSHIP EVER AGAIN.
That's it. I'm becoming a nun.
Really?
BUT I SURE AS HELL WASN'T GOING TO GIVE UP SEX.
no.

SO I BECAME A NUN WHO SLEPT AROUND.

AND THAT'S HOW LOVE HIT ME ON THE HEAD FOR THE THIRD TIME.

ONLY THIS TIME IT FELT LIKE A SLEDGEHAMMER.

JIM PLAYED THE GUITAR.

HE ALSO PLAYED WITH HIS FOOD.

AND HE PLAYED WITH ME.

HE LIKED MY TITS.

HE SEEMED TO THINK THEY BELONGED TO HIM.

HE'D HAD A VISION OF PARADISE SINCE HE WAS ABOUT TWELVE.

I JUST HOPED I WASN'T A DISAPPOINTMENT.

A disappointment?! You're my girlfriend! I love you!

Oh my God. He loves me.

I TRIED TO TELL MYSELF IT WASN'T THAT SERIOUS.

I mean, I'm a sophomore and he's about to graduate! How can it possibly be for real?

BUT IT WAS.

Listen. I don't mean to scare you, but I can see you two getting married. Seriously. And having a couple of kids.

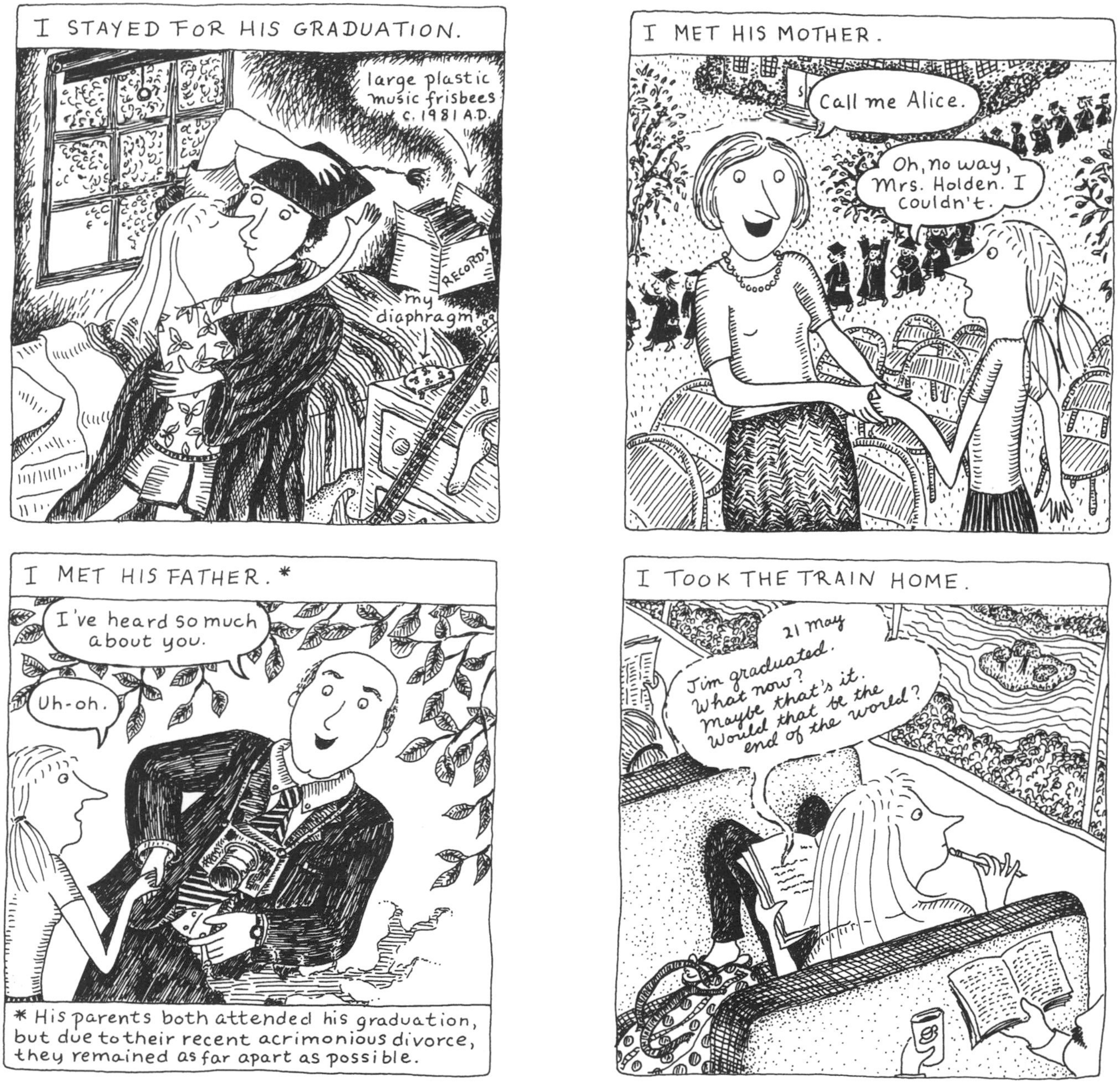
I STAYED FOR HIS GRADUATION.
large plastic music frisbees c. 1981 A.D.
RECORDS
my diaphragm
I MET HIS MOTHER.
Call me Alice.
Oh, no way, Mrs. Holden. I couldn't.
I MET HIS FATHER.*
I've heard so much about you.
Uh-oh.
* His parents both attended his graduation, but due to their recent acrimonious divorce, they remained as far apart as possible.
I TOOK THE TRAIN HOME.
21 may
Jim graduated.
What now?
maybe that's it.
Would that be the end of the world?

AND STAYED ON IT FOR TWO YEARS.

NOW AND THEN, I GOT OFF.

BUT I FELT MORE AT HOME ON THE TRAIN.

TRAVELING, I WAS NO ONE, JUST LIKE THE WOMAN NEXT TO ME.

WHEN I ARRIVED, I WAS—WHAT? A DAUGHTER?

A DAUGHTER-IN-LAW?*

* It can still be a wonderful relationship, even if you're not married to her son.

A LOVER?

*Yes, he still lived at home.

A GROUPIE?*

*This is why he still lived at home.

A STUDENT?

MAYBE IT HAD TO DO WITH GOING ON THE PILL.

ALL I KNEW WAS, FOR THE FIRST TIME IN MY LIFE, I COULDN'T GET ENOUGH TO EAT.

OR QUITTING SMOKING.

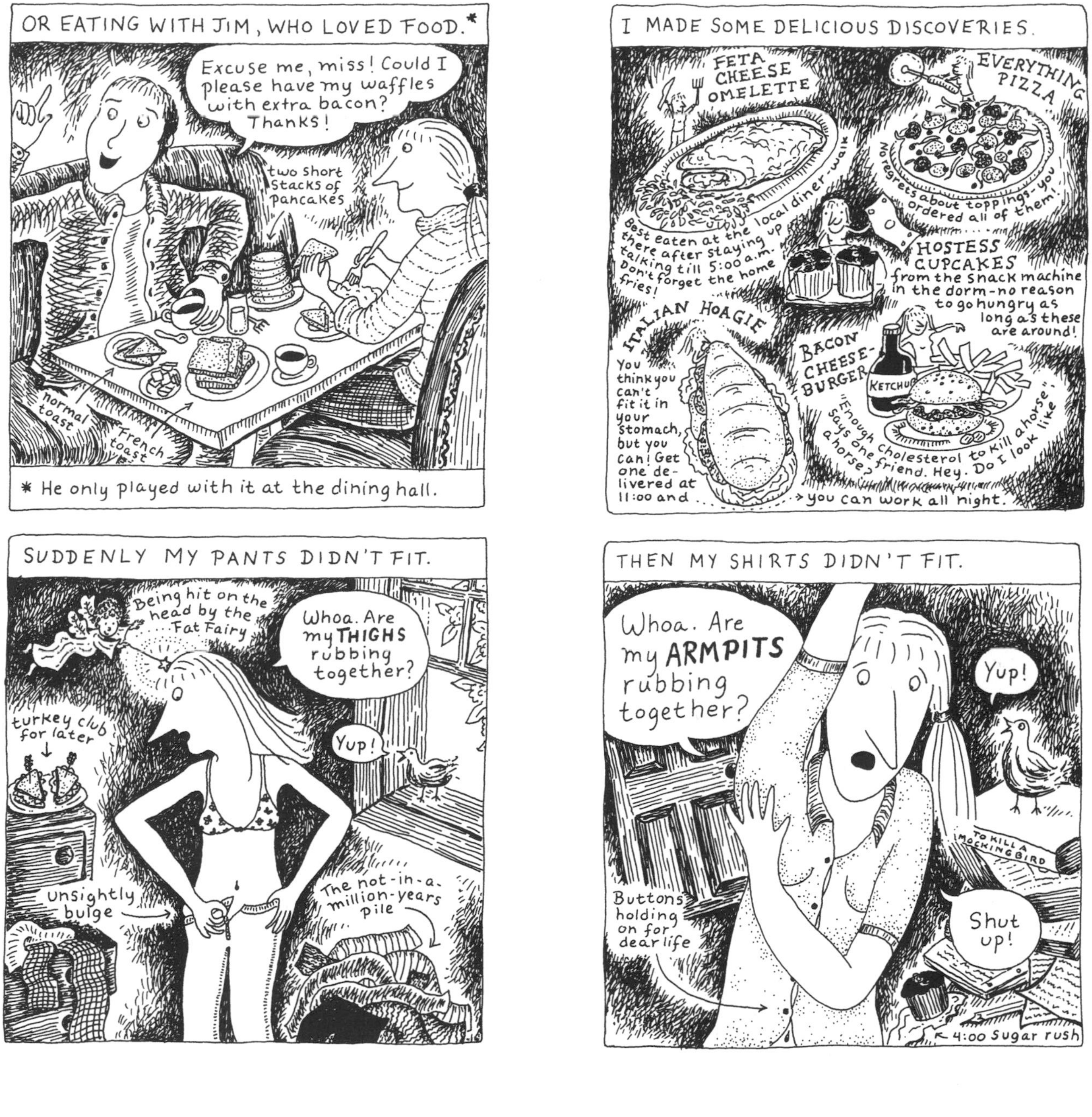
OR EATING WITH JIM, WHO LOVED FOOD.*
Excuse me, miss! Could I please have my waffles with extra bacon? Thanks!
two short stacks of pancakes
normal toast
French toast
* He only played with it at the dining hall.
I MADE SOME DELICIOUS DISCOVERIES.
FETA CHEESE OMELETTE
Best eaten at the local diner-walk there after staying up talking till 5:00 a.m. Don't forget the home fries!
EVERYTHING PIZZA
No regrets about toppings-you ordered all of them!
HOSTESS CUPCAKES
from the snack machine in the dorm-no reason to go hungry as long as these are around!
ITALIAN HOAGIE
You think you can't fit it in your stomach, but you can! Get one delivered at 11:00 and
you can work all night.
BACON CHEESE-BURGER
KETCHUP
"Enough cholesterol to kill a horse" says one friend. Hey. Do I look like a horse?
SUDDENLY MY PANTS DIDN'T FIT.
Being hit on the head by the Fat Fairy
Whoa. Are my THIGHS rubbing together?
turkey club for later
Yup!
Unsightly bulge
The not-in-a-million-years pile
THEN MY SHIRTS DIDN'T FIT.
Whoa. Are my ARMPITS rubbing together?
Yup!
TO KILL A MOCKINGBIRD
Buttons holding on for dear life
Shut up!
4:00 Sugar rush

AND ONE UNBELIEVABLE DAY, I REALIZED MY BRA WAS TOO SMALL.

AT LAST I HAD FULFILLED MY BIOLOGICAL DESTINY.

I WAS A 38C.

AND I HAD SOME SHOPPING TO DO.

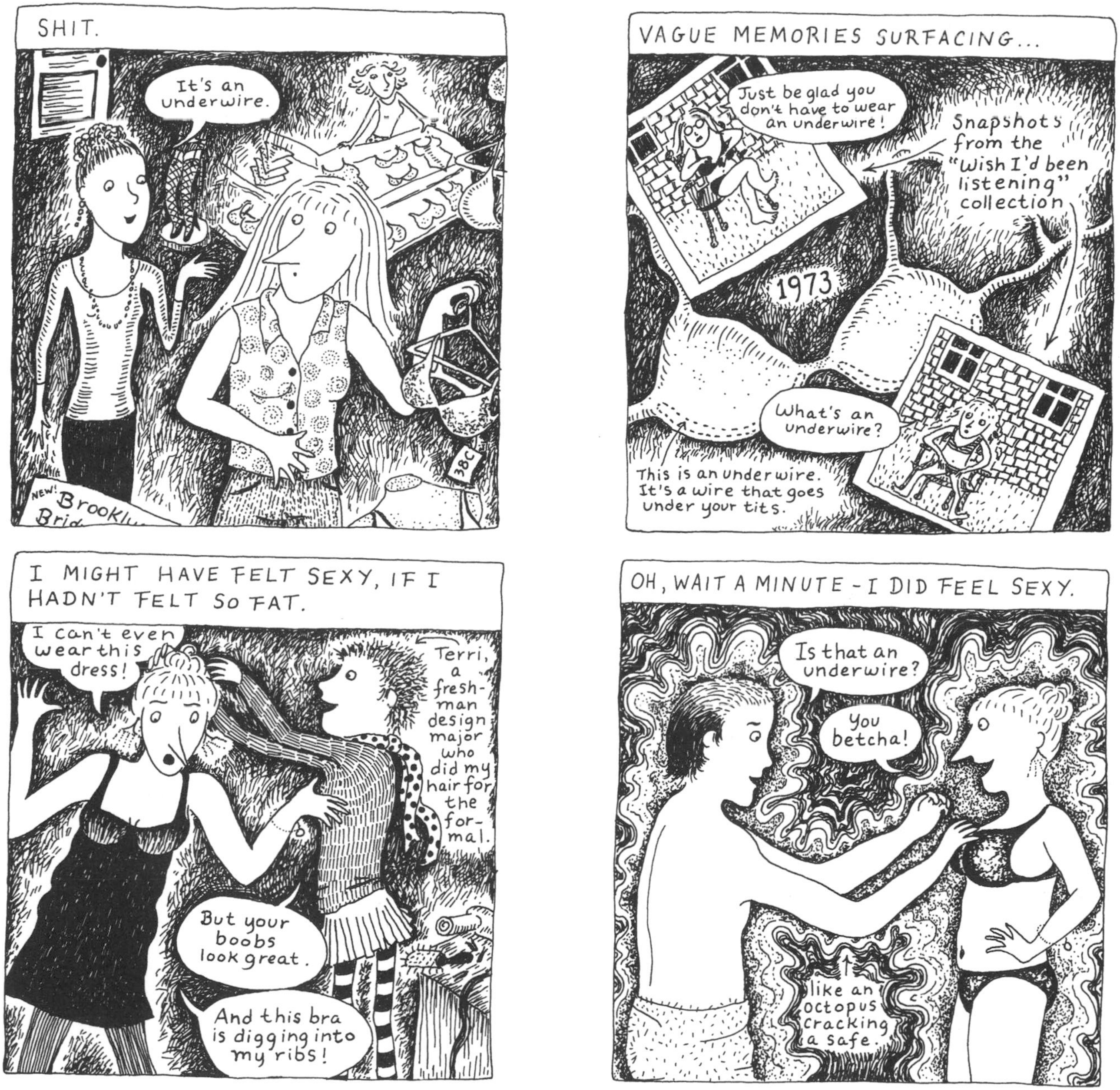
SHIT.
It's an underwire.
38C
VAGUE MEMORIES SURFACING...
Just be glad you don't have to wear an underwire!
Snapshots from the "Wish I'd been listening" collection
1973
What's an underwire?
This is an underwire. It's a wire that goes under your tits.
I MIGHT HAVE FELT SEXY, IF I HADN'T FELT SO FAT.
I can't even wear this dress!
Terri, a freshman design major who did my hair for the formal.
But your boobs look great.
And this bra is digging into my ribs!
OH, WAIT A MINUTE - I DID FEEL SEXY.
Is that an underwire?
You betcha!
like an octopus cracking a safe.

THEN ONE MORNING I WOKE UP AND IT WAS TIME TO GRADUATE.

JIM WAS THERE FOR ME.

AND MOM AND DAD CAME UP.

DAD HAD A BROKEN LEG.

THEY WERE ACTING WEIRD.

I DECIDED I DIDN'T WANT TO GO HOME WITH THEM.

I FELT A SLIGHT FOREBODING AS WE DROVE OFF INTO THE FUTURE.

TWO HOURS LATER, WE MISSED OUR EXIT.

CHAPTER FIVE:

SICK TITS

GET WELL SOON

THAT NIGHT I FOUND OUT WHY MOM AND DAD WERE ACTING WEIRD.

Your mother has a lump in her breast.

Bordeaux

COLD SWEAT CHILLED THE BACKS OF MY THIGHS.

WHAT?

DAD LOOKED HUGE. MOM LOOKED SO SMALL.

She's going into the hospital tomorrow for a lumpectomy. They'll biopsy it right there and if it's malignant she'll have a mastectomy.

Mom, shoulders up, defensive, protecting her poor breasts from the scalpel.

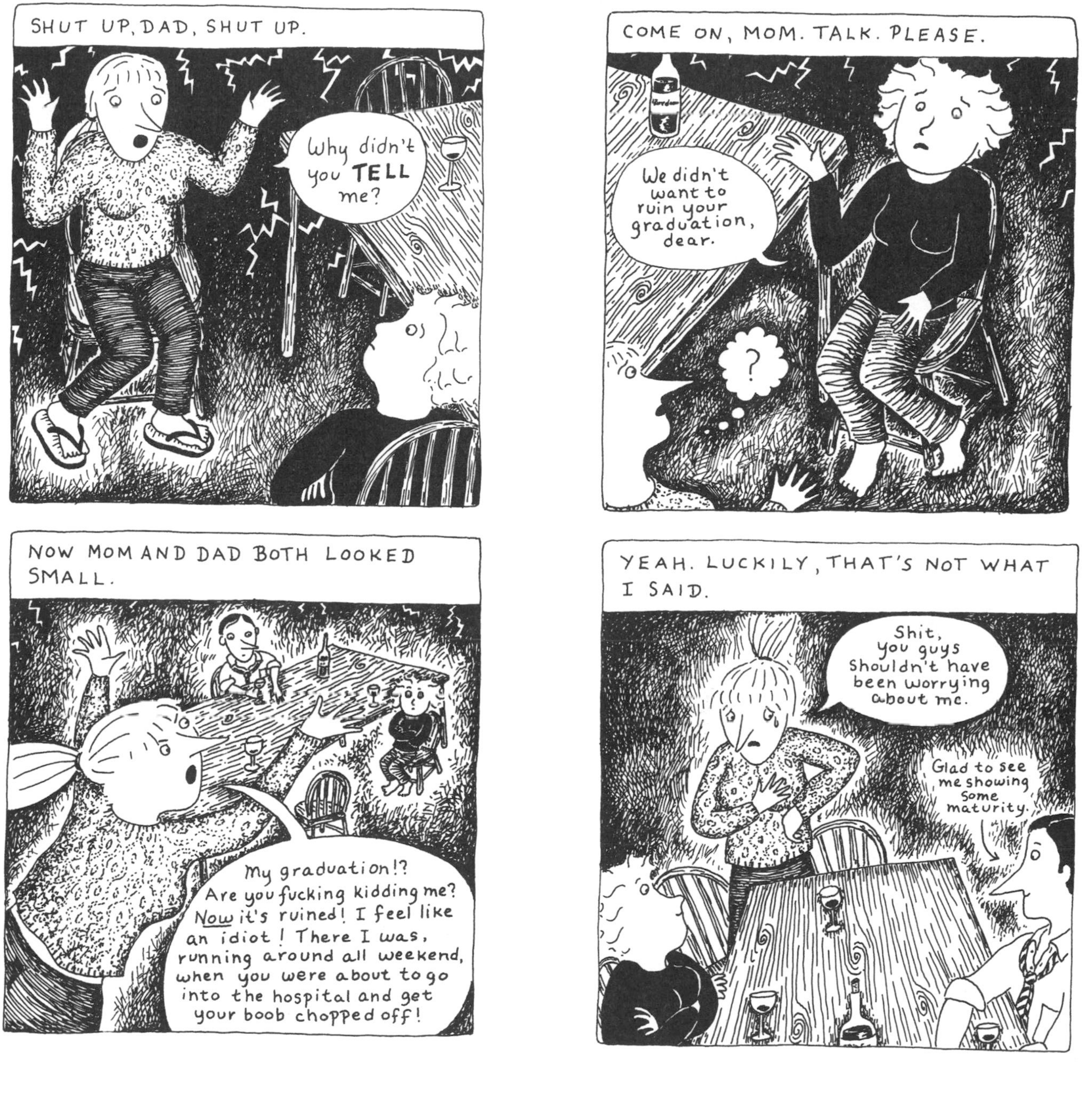
SHUT UP, DAD, SHUT UP.
Why didn't you TELL me?
COME ON, MOM. TALK. PLEASE.
We didn't want to ruin your graduation, dear.
?
NOW MOM AND DAD BOTH LOOKED SMALL.
My graduation!? Are you fucking kidding me? Now it's ruined! I feel like an idiot! There I was, running around all weekend, when you were about to go into the hospital and get your boob chopped off!
YEAH. LUCKILY, THAT'S NOT WHAT I SAID.
Shit, you guys shouldn't have been worrying about me.
Glad to see me showing some maturity.

I PATTED MOM'S BACK. I WANTED TO TOUCH HER.

I WANTED TO LET HER KNOW THAT I DIDN'T THINK I'D GET CANCER IF I TOUCHED HER.

AND I WANTED TO TOUCH HER BECAUSE DAD WASN'T TOUCHING HER.

AND I WANTED TO TOUCH HER BECAUSE SHE LOOKED SO UNTOUCHABLE.

SHE REMINDED ME OF A POEM WE READ IN SCHOOL ABOUT A DEER. *

* By Sir Thomas Wyatt, 1503 - 1542.

THE DEER IS A CHICK DEER AND SHE'S HARD TO GET.

SO HE MAKES UP AN EXCUSE TO QUIT CHASING HER.

HE SAYS SHE HAS A SIGN AROUND HER NECK SAYING, "DON'T TOUCH ME."

49

ONLY THE SIGN IS WRITTEN IN LATIN.

HERE'S THE INTERESTING PART—CHRIST SUPPOSEDLY SAID THESE WORDS TO HIS DISCIPLES AFTER HE ROSE FROM THE DEAD.

MY MOTHER SEEMED TO HAVE THIS SIGN AROUND HER NECK.

LIKE SHE WAS ALREADY DEAD.

LIKE I KILLED HER.

BUT SHE WASN'T DEAD YET. SHE JUST BELONGED TO DEATH.

I COULD THINK OF SO MANY TIMES I HAD HURT HER.

SHE HAD LOOKED INTO HIS UGLY FACE, AND NONE OF US HAD DONE THAT, SO SHE WAS IN A PLACE WHERE WE COULDN'T TOUCH HER.

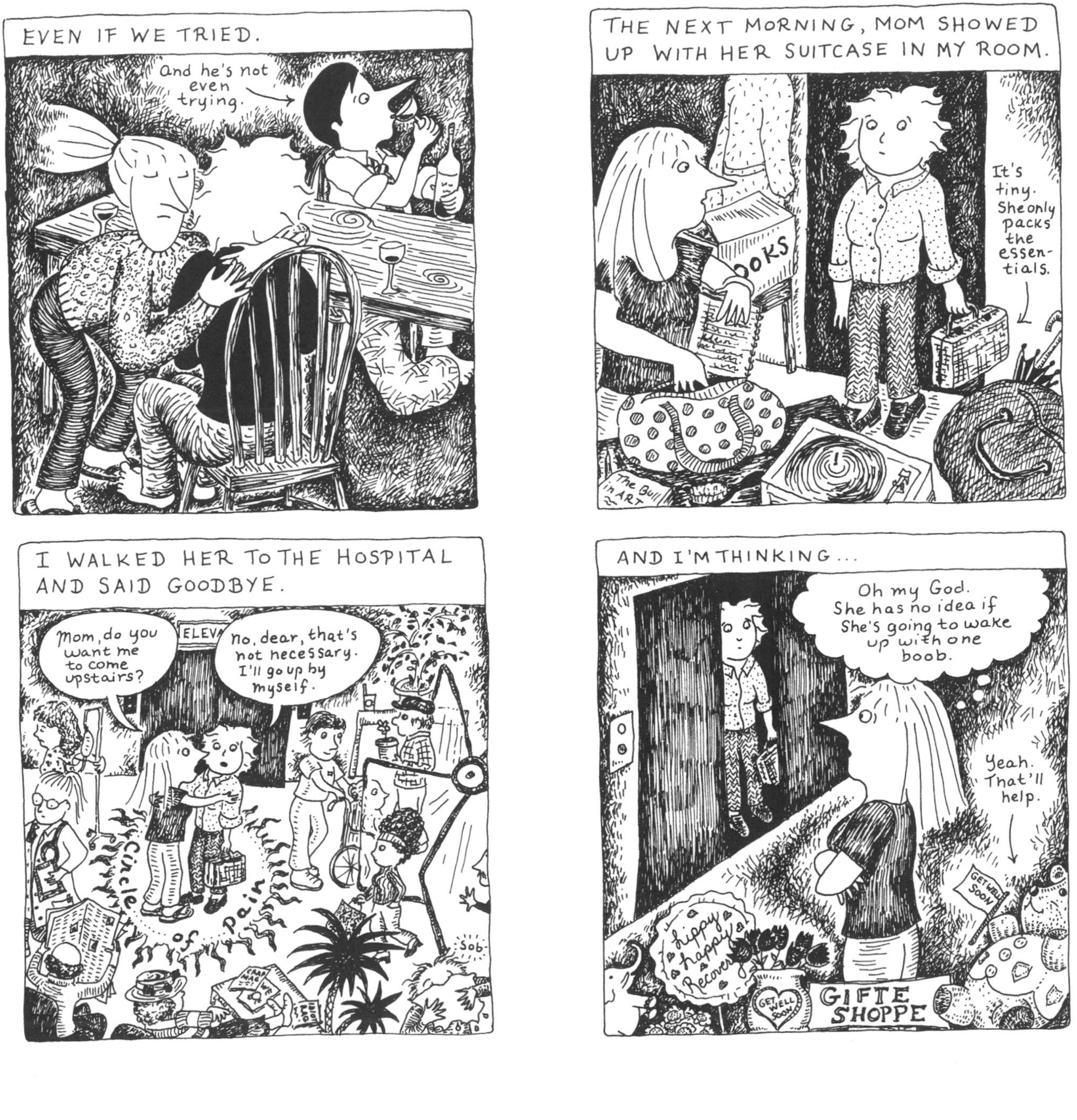
EVEN IF WE TRIED.
and he's not even trying.
THE NEXT MORNING, MOM SHOWED UP WITH HER SUITCASE IN MY ROOM.
It's tiny. She only packs the essen-tials.
BOOKS
The Bull in ART
I WALKED HER TO THE HOSPITAL AND SAID GOODBYE.
Mom, do you want me to come upstairs?
No, dear, that's not necessary. I'll go up by myself.
ELEVA
Circle of pain
Sob
AND I'M THINKING...
Oh my God. She has no idea if she's going to wake up with one boob.
Yeah. That'll help.
hippy happy Recovery
GET WELL SOON
GET WELL SOON
GIFTE SHOPPE

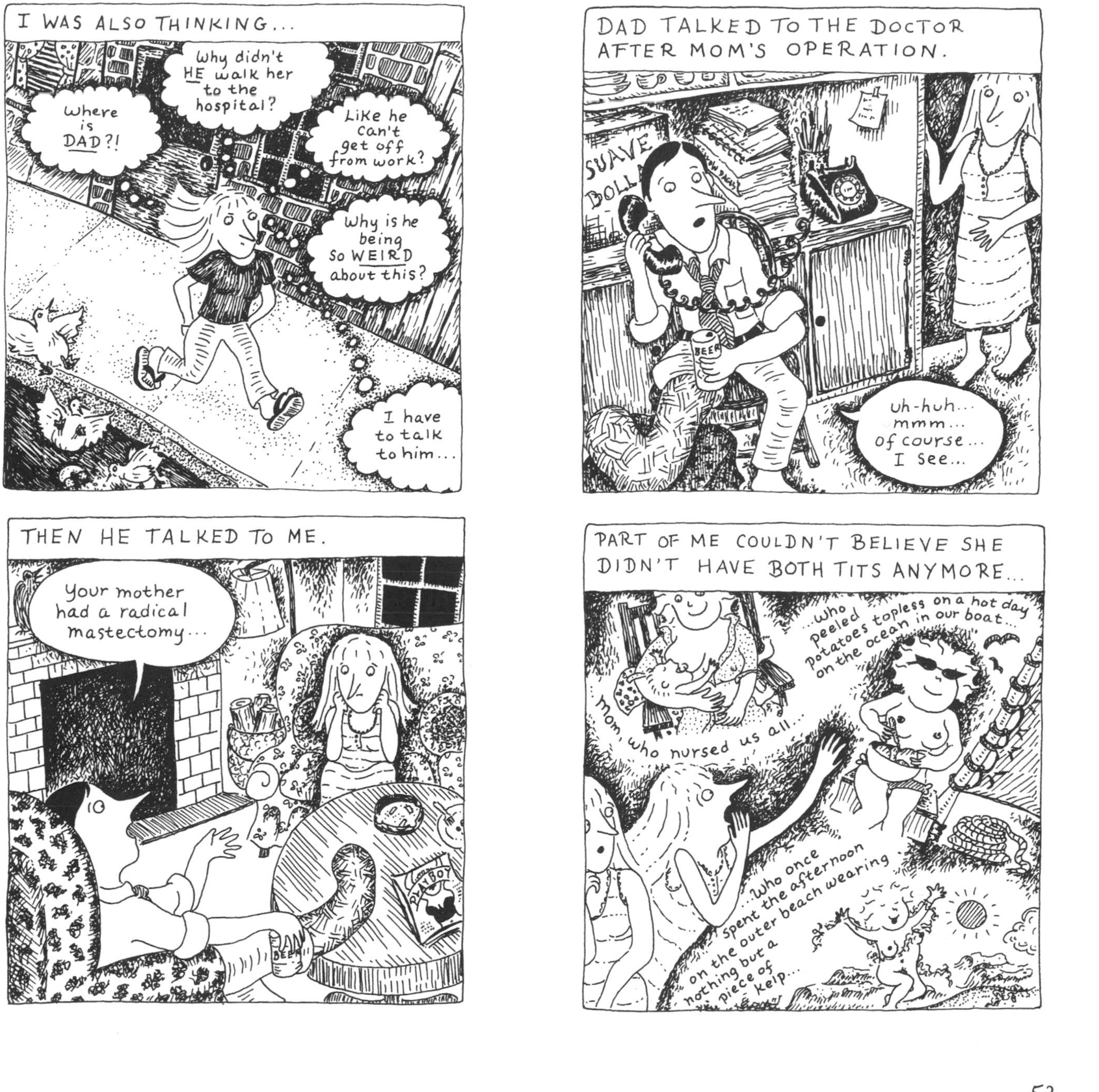
I WAS ALSO THINKING...
Where is DAD?!
Why didn't HE walk her to the hospital?
Like he can't get off from work?
Why is he being so WEIRD about this?
I have to talk to him...
DAD TALKED TO THE DOCTOR AFTER MOM'S OPERATION.
SUAVE
BEER
uh-huh... mmm... of course... I see...
THEN HE TALKED TO ME.
Your mother had a radical mastectomy...
PLAYBOY
BEER
PART OF ME COULDN'T BELIEVE SHE DIDN'T HAVE BOTH TITS ANYMORE...
Mom, who nursed us all...
...who peeled potatoes topless on a hot day on the ocean in our boat...
...who once spent the afternoon on the outer beach wearing nothing but a piece of kelp...

BUT ANOTHER PART OF ME WAS WONDERING WHY DAD, DURING THESE DISCUSSIONS, KEPT CALLING MOM "YOUR MOTHER".

HE WAS EXPLAINING HER OPERATION.

I ASKED WHY THEY HAD REMOVED HER LYMPH NODES.

THERE WAS A CERTAIN LACK OF UNDERSTANDING HERE ABOUT A LOT OF THINGS...

I WENT TO SEE MOM THE NEXT DAY.

THE RIGHT SIDE OF HER HOSPITAL GOWN WAS FLAT.

SHE WAS STILL GROGGY. AND SHE LOOKED SO SAD.

ALL MY LIFE I'D BEEN TRYING TO GET MY MOTHER TO TALK TO ME ABOUT HER EMOTIONS.

DAD WAS WILLING TO TALK ABOUT FEELINGS - HE JUST DIDN'T HAVE A HELL OF A LOT TO SAY.

DAD AND I WERE CLOSE, BUT STILL THERE WERE THINGS I WANTED TO TALK TO MY MOTHER ABOUT.

I WAS FIFTEEN AND A HALF: CALL THE FUCKING GUINNESS BOOK OF WORLD RECORDS.

God, I was so afraid I wasn't normal, Mom. All my friends got theirs in like sixth grade. I've been thinking maybe I didn't have a uterus.

Don't be silly, dear. Now would you please set the table?

WHAT REALLY HURT MY FEELINGS WAS THAT SHE DIDN'T WANT TO TALK ABOUT THEM EITHER.

Oh, and would you toss the salad for me?

Yeah. I'll toss the salad...

MY REVENGE WAS NEVER TO STOP TALKING ABOUT EMOTIONS — MINE AND EVERYONE ELSE'S.

UNLICENSED PSYCHOLOG 5¢

FREE BEER

THE DOCTOR IS IN

Holy shit! So how did you FEEL when your stepmother's lesbian lover came at you with the chainsaw?

NOW AND THEN I STILL TRIED TO CRACK MY MOTHER.

UNLICENSED PSYCHOLOGIST 5¢

THE DOCTOR IN

So mom, how did you feel, really, when your father died?

Well, not too happy, I suppose...

OR AT LEAST TELL HER MY PROBLEMS, SO SHE'D FEEL UP-TO-DATE.

Yeah, so I really love him, but **SHIT**, aren't I too young to be practically living with someone?

Uh...

AND ONE DAY, I WAS CERTAIN, SHE'D OPEN UP TO ME...

...And that's why I married your father.

Boy, you're right, honey. I do feel better talking about this stuff. Thanks for listening...

WHY NOT TODAY?

You've been through something really big, Mom. Don't you want to talk about it?

I HELD MY BREATH.

Well, I certainly don't think we need to **DWELL** on it.

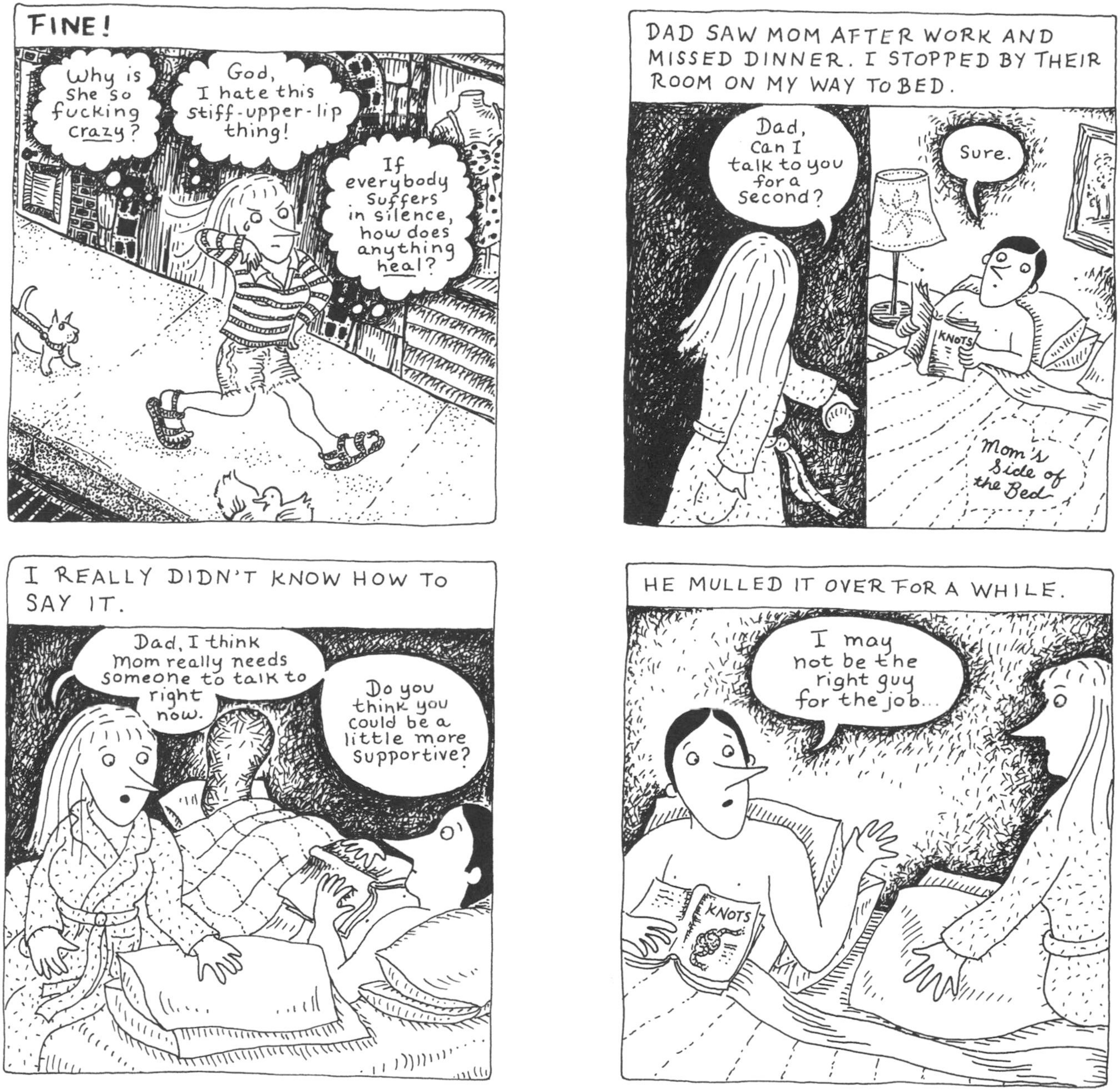
FINE!
Why is she so fucking crazy?
God, I hate this stiff-upper-lip thing!
If everybody suffers in silence, how does anything heal?
DAD SAW MOM AFTER WORK AND MISSED DINNER. I STOPPED BY THEIR ROOM ON MY WAY TO BED.
Dad, Can I talk to you for a second?
Sure.
KNOTS
Mom's Side of the Bed
I REALLY DIDN'T KNOW HOW TO SAY IT.
Dad, I think mom really needs someone to talk to right now.
Do you think you could be a little more supportive?
HE MULLED IT OVER FOR A WHILE.
I may not be the right guy for the job...
KNOTS

WHY THE FUCK NOT?
Well, what makes you think she wants to talk to me?
this is Mom
OH, I DON'T KNOW...
BECAUSE YOU'RE HER HUSBAND!
But I don't see how I can really help.
squeeze!
Poor Mom
squish!
KNOTS
EITHER MY FATHER WAS HIDING SOMETHING OR HE WAS AN EMOTIONAL PARAPLEGIC.
the doctor is in!
Dad. She's just lost one of her breasts. I'm sure she's worried you won't think she's sexy anymore. You can let her know you still, you know, love her.
Luv ya Mom
hug!
KNOTS
DAD LOOKED AT ME WITH HIS BIG BROWN EYES. THEN HE SAID SOMETHING REALLY WEIRD.
I know one thing for sure about your mother.
She's a survivor.
KNOTS
Squeeze!
What does THAT mean?

HE WAS RIGHT, THOUGH. WHEN I VISITED MOM THE NEXT DAY, SHE WAS ALREADY ON THE MEND. *

Next time you come, dear, would you bring me my sewing kit and the pair of your father's pants on my dresser?

Uh, Sure. Why?

* Get it? "On the mend"? Hoo boy!

SHE EVEN HAD ENOUGH ENERGY TO GET ON MY CASE.

I need to put a gusset in the leg of his pants so he can fit it over his cast...

You DO know what a gusset is?

Yes, mom! I know what a gusset is!

DON'T START WITH ME, YOU BITCH.

THE GUSSET:

a gusset

another fucking gusset

These suck.

my brother's old Levis miraculously TRANSFORMED into cool Bellbottoms by taking some fabric and adding GUSSETS!
GEE, THANX, MOM!

Yeah.

I GUESS YOU COULD SAY SEWING IS ONE OF THOSE SPECIAL THINGS MY MOTHER AND I NEVER SHARED...

I think the real question here is: why do you want to work on Dad's pants when you're lying in a hospital bed?

61

IT WAS A WALT DISNEY MOMENT.

SHE WAS CLINGING TO NORMALCY, AND THIS CONVINCED ME THAT SOMETHING REALLY FUCKED-UP WAS GOING ON.

I RACKED MY BRAINS.

SUDDENLY I REALIZED.

I USED TO HAVE THIS DREAM WHEN I WAS A KID WHERE I CAME HOME FROM SCHOOL AND MOM WAS ACTING FUNNY...

THEN DAD CAME HOME FROM WORK AND HE WAS ACTING FUNNY...

AND I KNEW THEY WEREN'T REAL — THEY WERE A ROBOT MOM AND DAD...

* I started swearing at a very early age.

AND OF COURSE I HAD TO BE SUPER-CAREFUL NOT TO SHOW THEM I'D NOTICED, SO THEY WOULDN'T KILL ME...

WHATEVER.

THERE WAS A LONG DELAY. HIS VOICE SOUNDED LIKE HE WAS YELLING DOWN A TUNNEL UNDER THE ATLANTIC.

I CALLED MY BROTHER, WHO WAS WORKING FOR A NEWSPAPER IN BRUSSELS.

I WISHED HE SOUNDED CLOSER.

64

HE WAS EITHER HYPERVENTILATING OR
BLOWING OUT CIGARETTE SMOKE.

Glad
I asked...

So how are
Mom and Dad
dealing
with it?

Oh, they're
fucked.
AS USUAL.

I REALIZED HE WAS TOO FAR AWAY FOR
US TO HAVE THE CONVERSATION I
REALLY WANTED TO HAVE.

Who knows.
I just think
they're acting
really
weird.

Well,
wouldn't
you? I mean,
Holy Shit!

I REALLY MISSED MY BROTHER'S
LIGHT-HEARTEDNESS. BUT HE WASN'T
MUCH OF A HAIR-SPLITTER...

Let's
get
drunk!

SO I CALLED MY SISTER, WHO WAS
IN VERONA, RESEARCHING HER
DISSERTATION.

Pronto?

hic!

marinara

Pasta
Fazool, man!
It's your
sister...

65

SHE WAS COOKING, WHICH IS WHAT SHE DOES WHEN SHE'S SUPPOSED TO BE WORKING.

HER VOICE SOUNDED CLOSER THAN MY BROTHER'S - BUT NOT BY MUCH.

THERE WAS ALSO A STRANGE TICKING ON THE LINE - LIKE A BOMB.

MY SISTER DIDN'T NEED WORDS TO EXPRESS HER FEELINGS ABOUT MY FATHER.

66

Panel 1:
HER NEXT WORDS, THOUGH, TELL YOU HOW CLOSE SHE IS TO MY MOTHER.

Well... They're not about to DWELL on it.

DID I SAY CLOSE, OR CLONE?

No...

BAD | GOOD
BUZZOMETER

But on the other hand, they could get together on this one, don't you think?

more Vin

Panel 2:
MY SISTER CLEARED HER THROAT.

Maybe not.

bzzz

hic! what do you mean?

OLD FRIEND

Panel 3:
THE TICKING ON THE LINE WAS GETTING LOUDER.

When I was staying at the apartment last summer, Dad was gone a lot...

Why?

zzzz

bzzz

Panel 4:
THE TICKING STOPPED.

nutella

Hey, it's their marriage, right?

hic?

67

KABOOM.

SO I CALLED JIM, WHO WAS LIVING IN PHILADELPHIA, WORKING FOR VARIOUS BANDS.

I CALLED HIM EVERY NIGHT, AFTER THE RATES WENT DOWN.

I COULD HEAR HIS GUITAR PLINKING WHILE HE PRACTICED, UNPLUGGED.

JIM HAD KNOWN MY FAMILY NOW FOR A COUPLE OF YEARS.

I think your Dad's a pretty serious skirt-chaser.

Art

COKE

He just likes women. It doesn't mean anything...

I'D BEEN EXPLAINING THIS TO PEOPLE SINCE I WAS THREE.

BEER

My Mommy says she doesn't care how many other ladies' boobies my Daddy looks at, because she trusts him.

ODDLY, NO ONE EVER SEEMED TO BUY IT.

Well, what about that time your Dad gave me a ride and we had to pick up his "friend" along the way?

So?

THERE WERE CERTAIN LADIES WHOSE BOOBIES MY FATHER LIKED MORE THAN OTHERS, AND THESE WOMEN BECAME FAMILY "FRIENDS."

He made me get in back so she could sit in the front seat.

COKE

So?

69

IT WASN'T POSSIBLE THAT WE'D ALL BEEN MISTAKEN—WAS IT?

MADNESS—AND A LOT OF RED WINE— WAS POUNDING IN MY EARS.

MOM CAME HOME.

SHE GAVE DAD HIS PANTS.

SHE ATE SOUP.

SHE ORDERED PROSTHETIC BRAS FROM A PLACE DOWN THE STREET.

HER TESTS CAME BACK.

I WANTED TO KNOW EXACTLY HOW HAPPY I SHOULD ALLOW MYSELF TO BE.

THIS WAS TRUE. BOTH MY PARENTS HAD A PHOBIA ABOUT TALKING ON THE PHONE. BUT STILL.

ONE PERSON - I CAN'T REMEMBER WHO - SAID:

72

IN THAT MOMENT I STRONGLY GRASPED THE EXTENT OF MY INTELLIGENCE AND EXPERIENCE.

LATER I PICKED UP THE PHONE TO CALL JIM, BUT THERE WAS —

— ALREADY A VOICE ON THE LINE.

A WOMAN'S.

SHE WENT SILENT.

MY FATHER'S VOICE JUMPED IN.

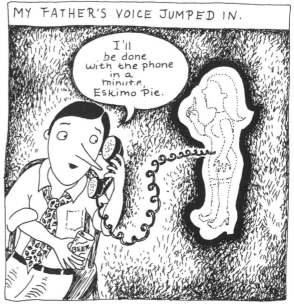

I'll be done with the phone in a minute, Eskimo Pie.

I HUNG UP.

MY BRAIN VOMITED A LIST OF PLAUSIBLE EXPLANATIONS:

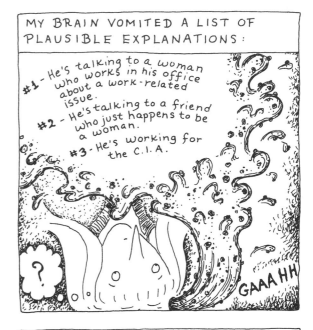

UPON CLOSER EXAMINATION, HOWEVER, THEY WEREN'T THAT PLAUSIBLE.

MOM WAS STILL UP.

SHE LOOKED AT ME. PISSED.

I KNEW THAT LOOK. *

* Please refer to page 31.

AND FINALLY I DID THE MATH.

PAMELA WAS DAD'S MOST RECENT "FRIEND", THE ONE HE'D DRIVEN HOME IN OUR CAR.

MOM DIDN'T SAY ANYTHING. SHE JUST KEPT GLARING AT ME.

BOY, SHE REALLY WAS NOT GOING TO MAKE THIS EASY FOR ME.

MY MOTHER SIGHED - AND OPENED UP AT LAST.

AND NOW THAT MY MOTHER HAD FINALLY OPENED UP TO ME, DID I OFFER HER MY FULL, UNCONDITIONAL, EMOTIONAL SUPPORT? FUCK NO.

OH RIGHT. I ALREADY PICKED UP ON THAT.

MOM HAD A FUNNY LOOK ON HER FACE - WAS THAT SHAME?

SHE SHRUGGED. GUILTY. AS IF I'D CAUGHT HER.

THERE WAS A DOOR WITH A GUY BEHIND IT, AND I WAS NEVER GOING TO STOP TALKING TO THE DOOR, WHICH WAS NEVER GOING TO OPEN. *

* Please refer to The Story of Hal, pages 32-33.

77

SO I PULLED THE GUY LIKE A SPLINTER FROM MY HEART. *

YANK!

* That is, once I had nothing left to say.

JUST TAKE THE TWEEZERS, MOM.

Mom? Why haven't you kicked him out?

HER ANSWER WAS FLINTY AND FINAL.

Inertia, I guess.

IT WAS LIKE THE PART IN A MOVIE WHERE THE CHARACTER YOU HAVE BEEN TRUSTING ALL ALONG TURNS OUT TO BE FUCKING NUTS.

INERTIA?

YOU GUESS??

You have to GUESS?

78

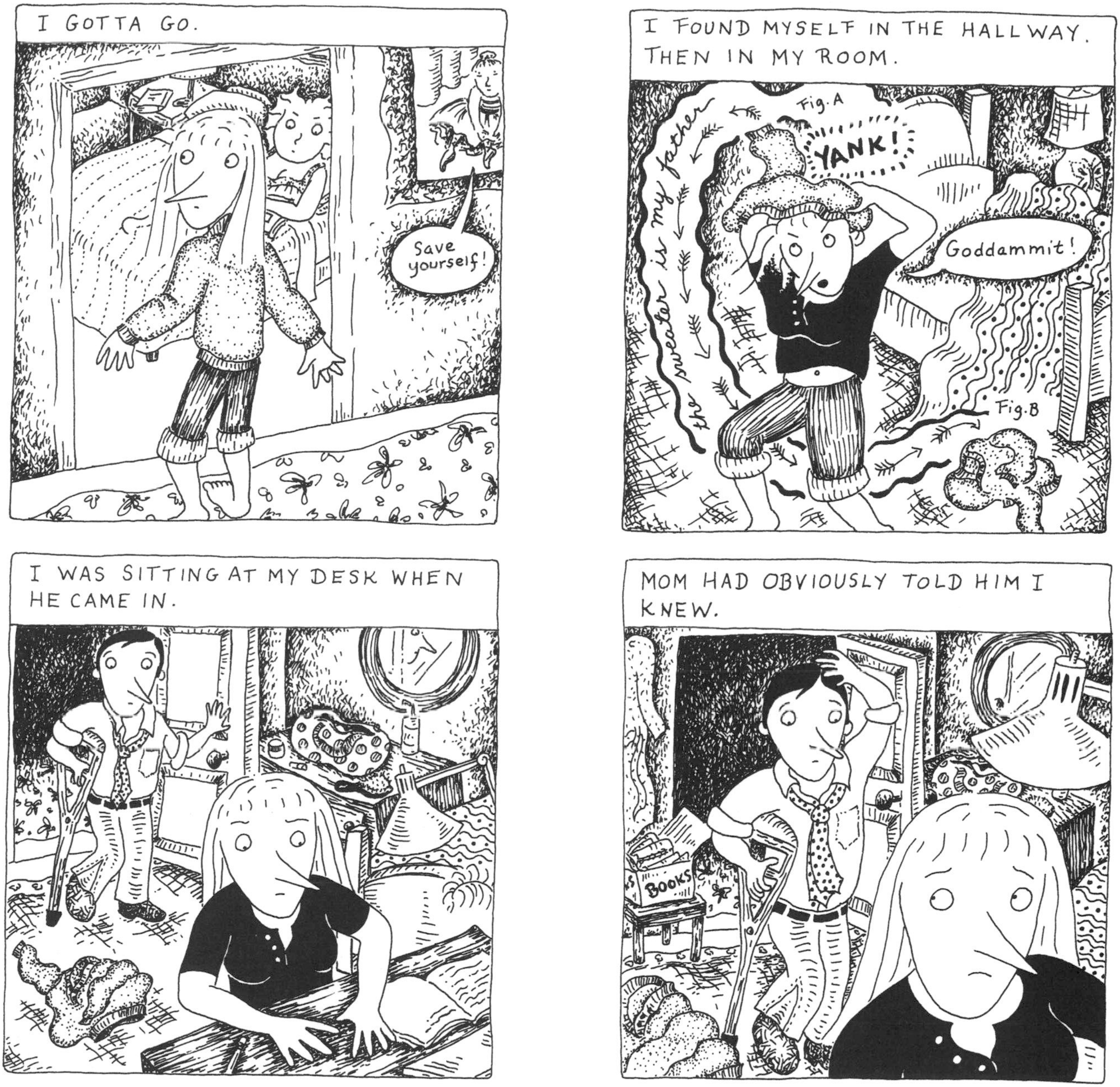
I GOTTA GO.
Save yourself!
I FOUND MYSELF IN THE HALLWAY. THEN IN MY ROOM.
Fig. A
YANK!
the sweater is my father
Goddammit!
Fig. B
I WAS SITTING AT MY DESK WHEN HE CAME IN.
MOM HAD OBVIOUSLY TOLD HIM I KNEW.
BOOKS

AND HE WANTED TO SAY SOMETHING. BUT HE HAD NO IDEA WHAT TO SAY...

SO HE WAITED FOR ME TO SAY SOMETHING INSTEAD. BUT I WAS TERRIFIED BY WHAT WAS GOING THROUGH MY HEAD.

SO NEITHER OF US SAID A WORD.

THEN I FELT HIS HANDS ON MY SHOULDERS. AND ALL I HAD TO DO WAS REACH UP AND TOUCH HIS FINGERS.

BUT I DIDN'T, AND AFTER A WHILE I FELT HIS HANDS SLIP AWAY AND HE WALKED OUT OF MY ROOM...
SAY Something! ANYTHING!!
JUST TURN AROUND AND LOOK AT HIM!
God, you cold cold BITCH!
AND THAT'S HOW I KILLED MY FATHER.
DAD
WORST THING I EVER DID.
AFTER THAT, A FIRE RAGED.
"HAPPY HOME"
"HONESTY"
COOKIE JAR
"HAPPY FAMILY"
GAS
"TRUST"
PLAYBOY

NOTHING SURVIVED.

EXCEPT—UNFORTUNATELY—ME.

THE QUESTION WAS: DID I WANT TO CONTINUE TO SURVIVE?

IF SO, THEN I'D BETTER MAKE A PLAN.

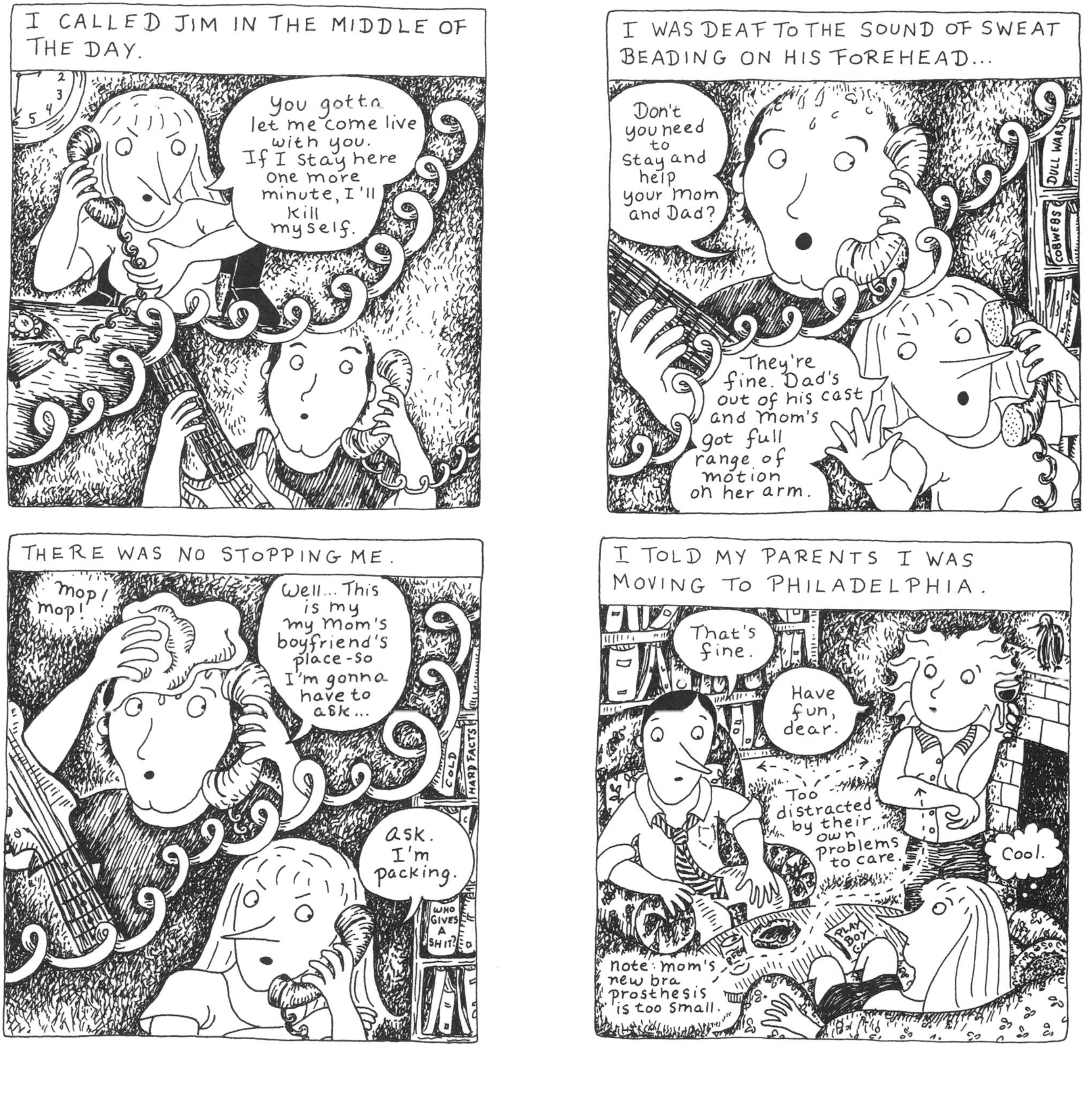
I CALLED JIM IN THE MIDDLE OF THE DAY.
You gotta let me come live with you. If I stay here one more minute, I'll kill myself.
I WAS DEAF TO THE SOUND OF SWEAT BEADING ON HIS FOREHEAD...
Don't you need to stay and help your Mom and Dad?
They're fine. Dad's out of his cast and Mom's got full range of motion on her arm.
DULL WARS
COBWEBS
THERE WAS NO STOPPING ME.
mop! mop!
Well... This is my my Mom's boyfriend's place-so I'm gonna have to ask...
Ask. I'm packing.
COLD
HARD FACTS
WHO GIVES A SHIT?
I TOLD MY PARENTS I WAS MOVING TO PHILADELPHIA.
That's fine.
Have fun, dear.
Too distracted by their own problems to care.
Cool.
PLAY BOY
note: mom's new bra prosthesis is too small.

WHILE I WAS PACKING, MY SISTER CALLED.

Mom says she's going to the Cape. I think you should go with her.

Trust me. I'm the last person she wants to be with.

ACTUALLY, MY FATHER WAS THE LAST PERSON SHE WANTED TO BE WITH.

Come on! She needs the company. Just for a month or so.

Listen! I've been here alone with Mom and Dad for the past six weeks and I can't do it anymore. They're **NUTS!**

MY SISTER GOT OUT THE SURGICAL INSTRUMENTS.

Do you really think she should be by herself right now?

OW!

PAIN!

OW!!

AGAIN, ALL I HAD TO DO WAS SAY I'D GO AND THE PAIN WOULD STOP.

I can't. I just can't.

AND THAT WAS THE OTHER WORST THING I EVER DID.

BUT HOW COULD I HAVE DONE ANYTHING ELSE? COLD DREAD WAS LICKING AT MY TOES...

A LOT OF SHIT WAS ABOUT TO GO DOWN, AND I WASN'T ABOUT TO GO DOWN WITH IT.

SO I SAVED MYSELF.

PLEASE, GOD, JUST LET ME GET OUT OF HERE IN ONE PIECE.

AND MAYBE TAKE A FEW THINGS WITH ME...

Diaphragm... lip gloss... journal.

I HESITATED ONLY A MOMENT AT THE TICKET WINDOW.

CLOSED

Philadelphia. One way.

NO PENNIES

Holy Shit! am I really going to live with a guy?

THEN I KEPT ON MOVING TOWARD THE LIGHT.

SCAMTRAK

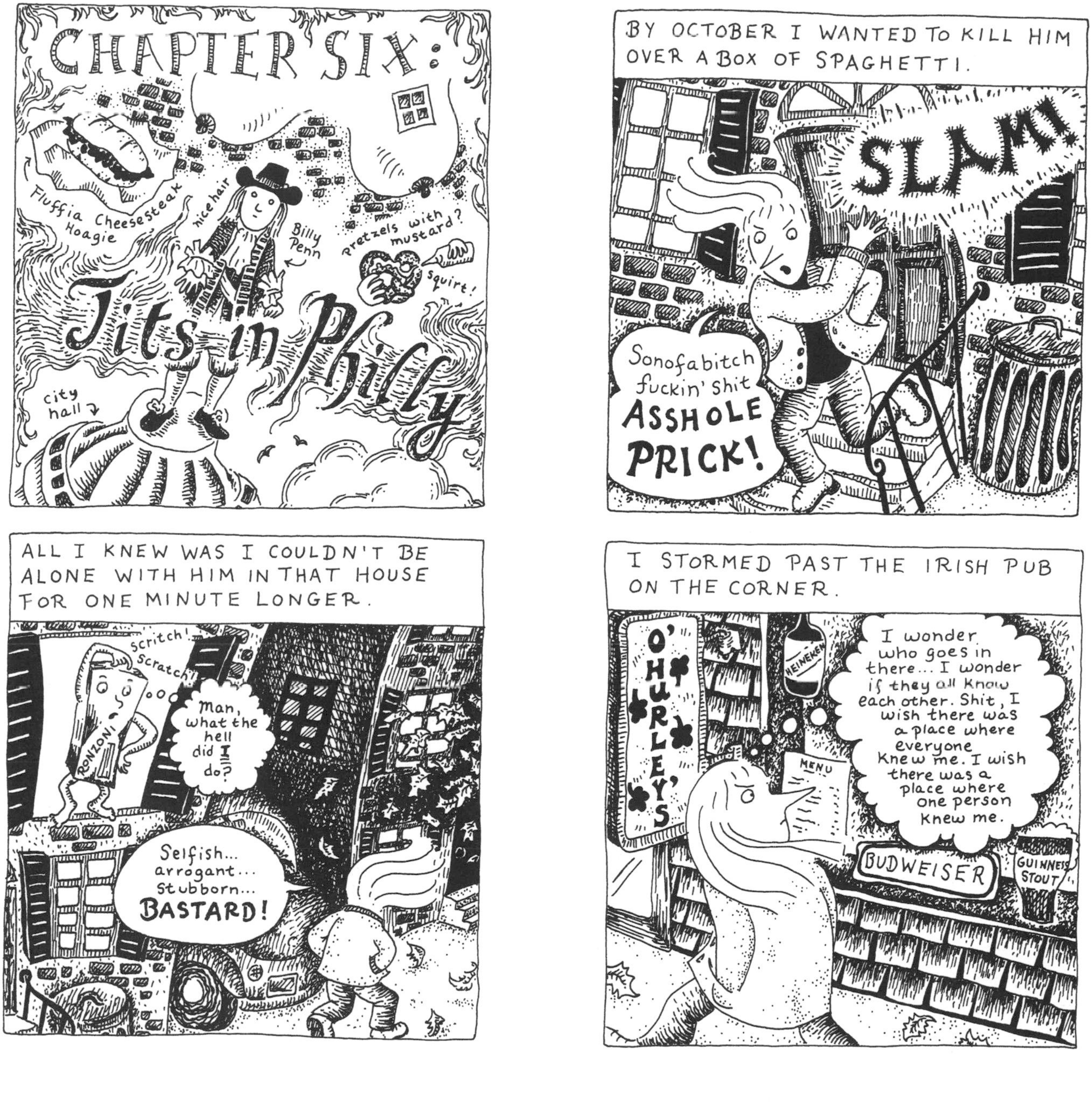
CHAPTER SIX:
Tits in Philly
Fluffia Cheesesteak Hoagie
nice hair
Billy Penn
pretzels with mustard?
squirt!
city hall
BY OCTOBER I WANTED TO KILL HIM OVER A BOX OF SPAGHETTI.
SLAM!
Sonofabitch fuckin' shit ASSHOLE PRICK!
ALL I KNEW WAS I COULDN'T BE ALONE WITH HIM IN THAT HOUSE FOR ONE MINUTE LONGER.
Scritch! Scratch!
RONZONI
Man, what the hell did I do?
Selfish... arrogant... stubborn... BASTARD!
I STORMED PAST THE IRISH PUB ON THE CORNER.
O'HURLEY'S
HEINEKEN
MENU
I wonder who goes in there... I wonder if they all know each other. Shit, I wish there was a place where everyone knew me. I wish there was a place where one person knew me.
BUDWEISER
GUINNESS STOUT

AND PETE'S PIZZA, WHICH WAS RESPONSIBLE FOR MY NEW FAT ASS.

ACTUALLY, MY ASS WAS FAT BECAUSE OF HOW GODDAMN MUCH I'D BEEN SITTING ON IT.

WHICH WAS JIM'S FAULT. HE WAS THE ONE WITH THE BRILLIANT IDEA THAT I SHOULD TAKE A YEAR OFF AFTER COLLEGE AND WRITE.

FUCK HIM FOR RESPECTING ME ENOUGH TO GIVE ME THE FIRST HONEST CHALLENGE OF MY LIFE.

88

NOT ONLY WAS THE FAT CREEPING ONTO MY THIGHS, BUT THE REALIZATION WAS CREEPING INTO MY SOUL THAT I SUCKED.

BUT I KEPT ON WORKING—I MEAN, SUCKING—SO THAT NOBODY WOULD FIND OUT THE TRUTH. I SUCKED FIVE OR SIX HOURS A DAY.

THE MARQUIS DE SADE COULD HAVE LEARNED A THING OR TWO FROM ME ABOUT PROLONGING THE FABULOUS AGONY OF SELF-INFLICTED PAIN.

* Translated from the French.

I READ SALVADOR DALI'S NOVEL ABOUT SADO-MASOCHISM AND FOUND A PHILOSOPHY THAT COULD GROW IN MY BURNED LANDSCAPE: SURREALISM.

THE MOST DISTURBING WAS GIORGIO DE CHIRICO, WHOSE PICTURES WERE LITTERED WITH SYMBOLS OF WHAT I DIDN'T WANT TO FEEL.

OH LOOK: HERE'S MY GUILT AND TERROR ABOUT WHAT THE DOCTORS (AND OTHERS) HAVE DONE TO MY MOTHER.

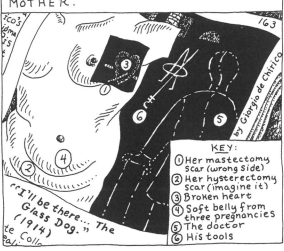

AND HERE'S MY FEAR OF ABANDONMENT, RIGHT WHERE I LEFT IT.

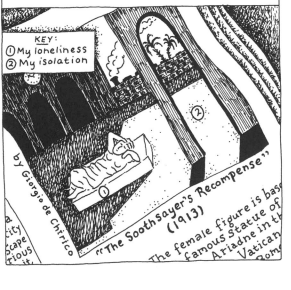

ARIADNE WOKE UP IN A STRANGE CITY, DITCHED BY THAT BASTARD THESEUS, AND SHE'D HURT HER PARENTS WAY TOO MUCH TO GO HOME.

SHE DREAMED CHILDHOOD DREAMS OF HER MOTHER AND FATHER, AS CONVINCED AS THIS GUY THAT SHE HAD LEFT SOMETHING THERE.

by Giorgio de Chirico

"The Child's Brain" (1914)

his fat

KEY:
① I have lost myself.
② Intellect is misleading.
③ I knew something when I was a child.

I DREAMED THESE DREAMS TOO. THEY WERE MYSTERIOUS AND SAD. I MADE AN EFFORT TO UNDERSTAND THEM.

What...

Shut up! Shut up! I'm trying to remember something. Oh fuck, what **WAS** that?

I DREAMED MY OLD RECURRENT NIGHTMARE ABOUT THE RED HALL.

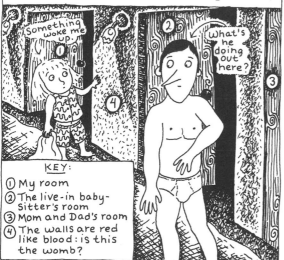

Something woke me up.

What's he doing out here?

KEY:
① My room
② The live-in baby-sitter's room
③ Mom and Dad's room
④ The walls are red like blood: is this the womb?

MOM CAME OUT OF THEIR ROOM AND LOOKED DOWN THE HALL, QUESTIONING HIM TOO.

Now I'm scared

Were you doing something in the babysitter's room?

Well, were you?

91

CALM AND INNOCENT, HE LOOKED HER IN THE EYES. AND I SAW HER HESITATE.

THEN EVERYTHING WAS OKAY, AND MOM TURNED, AND DAD FOLLOWED HER TO BED.

SO DID I KNOW SOMETHING I DIDN'T KNOW I KNEW?

I DREAMED A NEW NIGHTMARE TOO, IN WHICH I WAS A CHILD.

MY MOTHER AND FATHER WERE DEAD.

I RAGED MY WAY DOWN TO THE PARK ON THE RIVER.

THEN I STOPPED - BECAUSE I HAD NOWHERE ELSE TO GO.

WHEN I TURNED AROUND, THIS WEIRD GUY WAS TRAINING HIS DOG.

I THOUGHT: WOW, IT'S ALL ABOUT POWER. NO, NOT POWER. STRENGTH. AND WHICH TAKES MORE STRENGTH, LEAVING OR STAYING?

NO, NOT STRENGTH. DISCERNMENT. ONE WAY WAS THE FUTURE, ONE WAY WAS THE PAST. THE ONLY THING I KNEW ABOUT MY FUTURE WAS HIM.

I WALKED UP THE STAIRS TO THE KITCHEN.

DON'T PLAY MISTER FUCKING INNOCENT WITH ME.

LOOK AT THAT: HE'D MADE THE SPAGHETTI - AND A SALAD...

HOME.

HE STOPPED CUTTING.

LOVE, IN THE MIDDLE OF A STRANGE LAND.

LATER, WE WERE UPSTAIRS WATCHING TV.

HE FLICKED OFF THE LIGHTS.

HE LEFT THE ROOM FOR A MOMENT.

HE WAS LOOKING AT THE GIRLS' DORMITORY OF AN ART COLLEGE ACROSS THE STREET. I OFTEN WONDERED WHAT THEY WERE UP TO OVER THERE.

WHAT WAS IT LIKE, MAKING ART ALL DAY? HOW DID THEY COME UP WITH THEIR IDEAS?

Here. Look.

Fine. Pervert.

AND THIS GIRL—WAS SHE HAPPY, LIVING IN HER OWN ROOM, GOING TO CLASS, PAINTING, MAKING TIME WITH THIS GUY?

I FELT JIM'S FINGERS CLOSE OVER MY BREASTS AND SQUEEZE THEM.

I bet she doesn't have a rack like this, though.

Stairs

COKE

trash

THE WINDOW ACROSS THE STREET WENT DARK.

Great. I've got tits, but no life.

97

IN JUNE, WE MOVED BACK TO JIM'S MOTHER'S PLACE.

SHE HAD AN OLD FARM IN THE SMALL TOWN OF BOSKY DELL, NEW JERSEY.

WE WERE "HOUSESITTING" WHILE SHE AND HER BOYFRIEND WORKED IN PHILLY.

THEY STAYED AT HIS PLACE (OUR OLD ADDRESS) DURING THE WEEK AND CAME OUT HERE ON WEEKENDS.

THERE WAS PLENTY OF ROOM FOR EVERYBODY.

AND I DO MEAN EVERYBODY.

BUT I TOOK UP LESS SPACE NOW THAN I DID IN PHILADELPHIA.

99

BOY WAS THAT GUY SURPRISED...

BUT IT WAS OKAY, BECAUSE NOW I WAS LIVING IN THE LAND OF MEN.

JIM'S BROTHER DREW WAS A COMPUTER NERD WHO COULD FIX ANYTHING.

One year younger than Jim, Drew got a master's in computer science.

Drew got a computer research job in Jersey for a while and moved in with us at his mom's.

He built a computer lab in the barn, upstairs, where he developed his own software.

He also built a Jaguar from scratch in the barn, downstairs.

Drew was a pretty hands-on guy.

PAUL, THE NEXT BROTHER DOWN, WAS A REALLY FRIENDLY GUY WITH A FLAIR FOR DECORATING.

He grew these:

He bought the vases. (antiques)

After a while, he settled in Jersey, working in historic preservation and living with us at his mom's.

Paul finished college and then went to graduate school, getting a degree in decorative arts and coming home every weekend to do his laundry.

If Paul was home, no one had to mow the lawn or water the gardens or trim the hedges or prune the trees, etc.

You could really talk to Paul.

DAN, THE YOUNGEST, WAS A COMPUTER GEEK WITH HINTS OF JOCK AND PARTY BOY.

Dan came home for vacations while he finished college in California.

He liked to design hallucinogenic computer programs and read Calvin & Hobbes.

One time he was reaching for a cupboard in the kitchen and I noticed his perfect abs and this little part of me almost passed out...

abs: Down, girl!

He got a computer job in Jersey too and lived with us at his mom's before going to Michigan to get his master's.

WHEN I MET JIM'S BROTHERS IN COLLEGE, I NEEDED OXYGEN.

Bachelor #1

Bachelor #2

Bachelor #3

Uh... hi.

Hey!

Hey there!

Three backups — and they're all gorgeous!

LIVING WITH THEM WAS AN ENTIRELY DIFFERENT THING.

IT WAS NOT WITHOUT AN ELEMENT OF RISK.

FIRE. WATER. WHATEVER.

THEY HAD AN INSTANT LIKING FOR ANYTHING THEY COULD BLOW UP.

ONE NIGHT DREW CAME HOME WITH THIS COOL NEW THING CALLED A VCR.

DREW, WHO SEEMED TO BE GOING THROUGH A ROUGH PATCH, BROUGHT HOME A SLASHER MOVIE EVERY NIGHT AFTER THAT.

THEN DREW STARTED BUYING CHEAP PLASTIC BABY DOLLS, INJECTING THEM WITH SHAVING CREAM AND RED FOOD COLORING, AND...

THEY HAD NAMES...

BABY SALEM WITCH HUNT WAS BURNED AT THE STAKE.

THEY POURED A LINE OF GASOLINE DOWN THE DRIVEWAY, PLACED SOME CAPS AT ONE END, AND SHOT THE CAPS WITH A BB GUN.

THEN THEY WENT BACK INSIDE TO FINISH UP THEIR VIDEO MARATHON OF DEATH WISH ONE, TWO, AND THREE.

THAT WAS THE ONLY TIME I FELT A LITTLE UNSAFE.

MOSTLY I FELT CHALLENGED — TO BE AS FEARLESSLY AND ENERGETICALLY MYSELF AS THEY WERE.

But how?

Step One: Put on your pants.

AND THAT'S WHERE JIM'S MOTHER CAME IN.

reading glasses

Oh, I love those. They make you look so skinny. What else did you get?

Oh, lots of stuff. I'll show you.

new pants

THE LAND OF MEN WAS PRESIDED OVER BY A WOMAN WHO WAS STRONGER THAN ALL OF THEM.

I told the board-members I'm resigning because it's a crock of shit!

Wow.

FILE

I TRIED TO RESIST HER FRIENDSHIP AT FIRST, ON PRINCIPLE.*

Have dinner with me. Tell me what you're writing about these days...

Oh no you don't. If you and I like each other too much, Jim will feel obligated to stay with me, and I'm not that kind of girl.

*This was back in Philadelphia.

BUT NOW THAT I WAS LIVING WITH A MAN — MEN — WHAT I WANTED MOST DESPERATELY WAS A WOMAN.

ACTUALLY, WHAT I REALLY WANTED WAS AN OLDER WOMAN, AND I BELIEVE SHE WANTED A YOUNG ONE.

SHE TOLD ME HOW IT FELT WHEN HER FATHER DIED, WHEN HER MARRIAGE CRUMBLED, WHEN SHE FELL IN LOVE AGAIN WITH HER BOYFRIEND FORD.

THERE WERE TIMES WHEN EVEN I COULDN'T KEEP UP WITH HER BOTTOMLESS INTEREST IN OTHER PEOPLE.

BUT WHEN WE VISITED THE TOWN SHE'D GROWN UP IN, I BEGAN TO UNDERSTAND.

That's the house I lived in with my mother and father.

And this is the cemetery where I used to play, across the street.

SERIOUSLY?

Mrs. Holden, that's so sad.

Oh, no it wasn't. I liked it here. And this was my favorite...

SHE WALKED OVER TO A HEADSTONE.

The lambs. I used to feed them.

BECAUSE THAT'S WHO SHE WAS— THE GIRL WHO'D GIVE LOVE TO A STONE.

Eat, Lamby. It's nice fresh grass.

MARY 1893-1895 OUR LITTLE LAMB

AT THIS STRANGE MOMENT IN MY LIFE, MRS. HOLDEN—LOVINGLY— MADE A SUGGESTION.

Why don't you get a job?

I ALREADY HAD A PART-TIME JOB AT THE LOCAL PHARMACY, BUT I HATED IT.

Ned, the pervert slash pharmacist

Kill me. NOW.

Dawn, tenth grader who is better at this job than I am

NO PERSONAL CHECKS!

muzak that makes me wonder if I am stuck inside the set of a soap opera and will NEVER GET OUT!

nancy, the fugly makeup lady

SHE MEANT A WRITING JOB.

A friend of mine has her own public relations firm. She might need a writer. Why don't you give her a call?

Okay.

AND SO I COMPLETED MY MAKEOVER FROM ANGRY FAT-ASSED SURREALIST TO PERKY THIN SURREALIST, ASSISTANT TO THE HEAD OF THE FIRM.

What the FUCK are you doing?

No shit! Do you really think you're the business type?

Oh, just take their money until they find out how incompetent you are!

hope

I GOT A JACKET WITH SHOULDER PADS.

I GOT A BRIEFCASE.

I GOT LEOPARD-PRINT HIGH-HEELED SHOES.

BEST OF ALL, I GOT PAID—AND NOT JUST MINIMUM WAGE.

I TRIED TO SOUND CASUAL, BUT I'D BEEN HAVING DREAMS...

You know, we don't have to live with your mother anymore. We could think about getting our own place.

IN ONE DREAM, WE MOVED INTO A TREEHOUSE.

Well, there's not much space, but it's got a great view.

I guess it'll get a little cold this winter...

JIM - CLEARLY - HAD NOT BEEN HAVING THE SAME DREAMS.

Are you out of your mind? What kind of place do you think we can afford?

I don't know. Something small and crappy.*

* You know - like a treehouse.

HE WAS FURIOUS.

You go ahead and let me know how it turns out.

Oh, come on! I don't want to move out alone - I want to move out with you!

plunk!

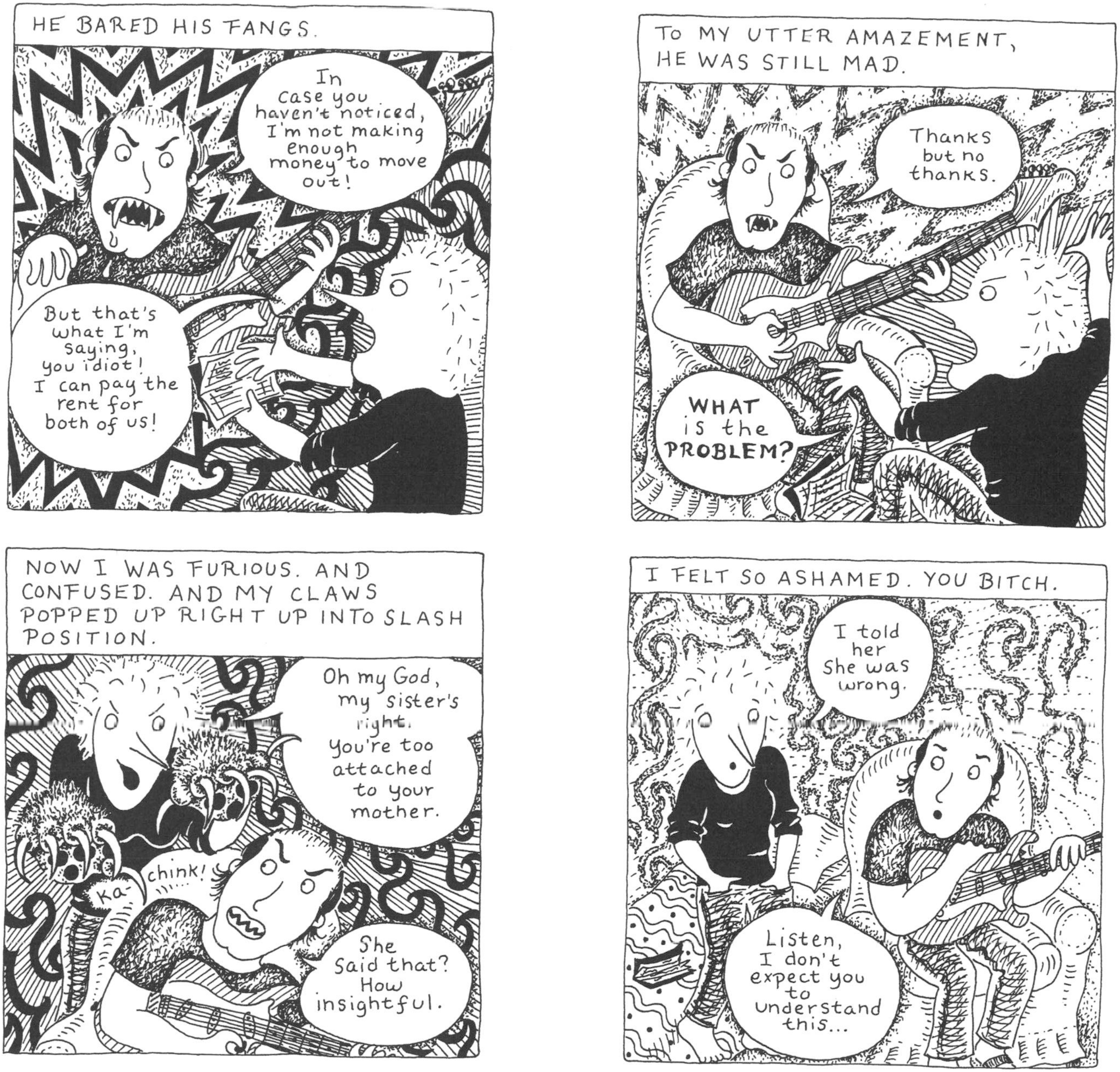
HE BARED HIS FANGS.
In case you haven't noticed, I'm not making enough money to move out!
But that's what I'm saying, you idiot! I can pay the rent for both of us!
TO MY UTTER AMAZEMENT, HE WAS STILL MAD.
Thanks but no thanks.
WHAT is the PROBLEM?
NOW I WAS FURIOUS. AND CONFUSED. AND MY CLAWS POPPED UP RIGHT UP INTO SLASH POSITION.
Oh my God, my sister's right. You're too attached to your mother.
Ka-chink!
She said that? How insightful.
I FELT SO ASHAMED. YOU BITCH.
I told her she was wrong.
Listen, I don't expect you to understand this...

HE PUT DOWN HIS GUITAR.

SPARKS FLEW OFF HIM.

BUT I WANTED THE GUY WHO NEVER BROKE A PROMISE TO ANYBODY, NOT EVEN HIMSELF.

HIS NECK SMELLED SO SWEET.

IT WAS TIME FOR A VISIT FROM THE STORK.

WE CALLED HIM ICKY, SHORT FOR ICHABOD CRANE.

AND WE SPOILED HIM.

SUDDENLY I WAS HOLDING A HANDFUL OF WILDFLOWERS IN THE MIDDLE OF MY SISTER'S WEDDING.

AND I WAS WONDERING: HOW THE HELL DID THIS HAPPEN?

- HIC!

So then she throws up all over my shoes—well, they were her shoes, actually—and she passes out, and I have to figure out how to drag her ass back to her college apartment at four o'clock in the morning...

MY BROTHER WAS SITTING THERE WITH HIS WIFE.

I mean, what is this Adulthood thing? Is there some metal detector I'm going to have to walk through and if I'm not married and don't have my own place, it'll go off? BEEP!

hic!

hic! rrrp!

always drunker than I am →

MOËT

SHE'S JUST LIVING WITH THE GUY SHE'S GOING TO SPEND THE REST OF HER LIFE WITH. BEEP!

- hic!

And what the hell difference does marriage really make? I mean, look at Mom and Dad!

drunken of pantyhose removal

Sometimes I just had to bum a butt

hic!

NOBODY WANTED TO LOOK AT MOM AND DAD.

THEY WERE MISERABLE.

Dad forgetting to set his watch—just staring into space, wondering how long he can divide his time between his wife and comfortable home, and his girlfriend Pamela in her tiny apartment across town...

TWO YEARS HAD PASSED AND THEY STILL HADN'T SEPARATED.

Mom recognizing Pamela's number on the phone bill she's in the middle of paying, wondering how long she can divide her heart between being scorned and humored by a guy who's her husband in name only...

WHAT WERE THEY WAITING FOR—A SIGN FROM GOD?

Thou shalt get a Divorce, already! Oy!

WHOA! Holy shit! You guys got kicked out AGAIN?

MEANWHILE, WE WERE ALL SUPPOSED TO ACT AS IF NOTHING HAD HAPPENED.

WHICH MADE ME SO ANXIOUS THAT WHEN I WAS ALONE WITH THEM MY HEART WOULD RACE, MY PALMS WOULD SWEAT, AND I'D START HALLUCINATING.

MOM WAS BLEEDING FROM HER EYES, AND FROM HER MASTECTOMY WOUND, WHICH HAD NOT HEALED.

THERE WAS AN ELEPHANT IN THE ROOM.

AND DAD WAS RIDING IT.

116

AND IT WAS TRAMPLING MOM UNDERFOOT.

I OPENED MY MOUTH TO SHOUT, BUT ONLY A DEEP MOAN CAME OUT, DEAFENING, ERASING ALL OTHER SOUND.

MY BROTHER AND I GOT ON THE END OF A LINE OF PEOPLE PASSING A JOINT.

So you're saying, what's the difference. Between living together and getting married.

I seriously need to be fuckin' elucidated.

I'll tell you. What it is.

nice tits, man!

thanks.

hic!

MY BROTHER ALWAYS GREW MORE PERCEPTIVE AS THE NIGHT BOOZED ON.

When you get married, there's no trap door.

hic!

hic!

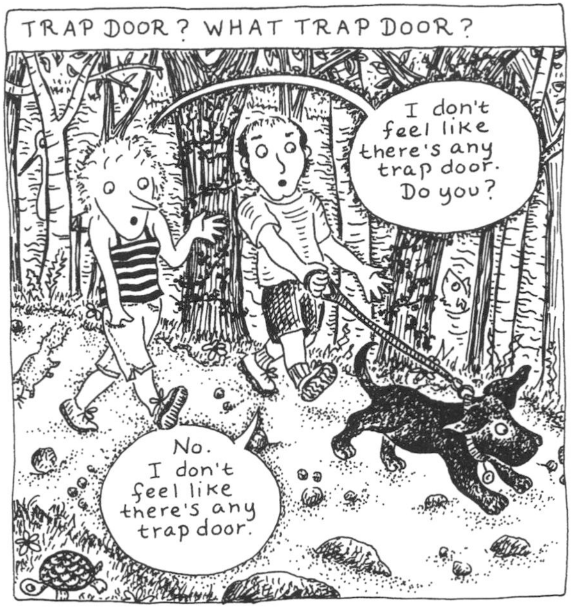
TRAP DOOR? WHAT TRAP DOOR?
I don't feel like there's any trap door. Do you?
No. I don't feel like there's any trap door.

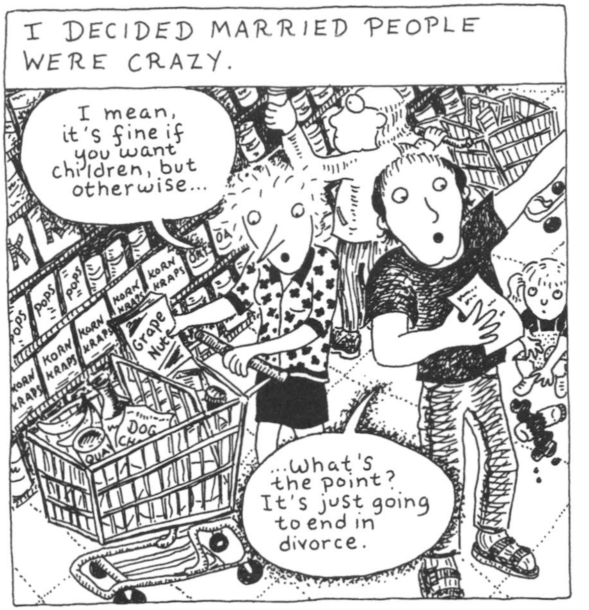
I DECIDED MARRIED PEOPLE WERE CRAZY.
I mean, it's fine if you want children, but otherwise...
...What's the point? It's just going to end in divorce.

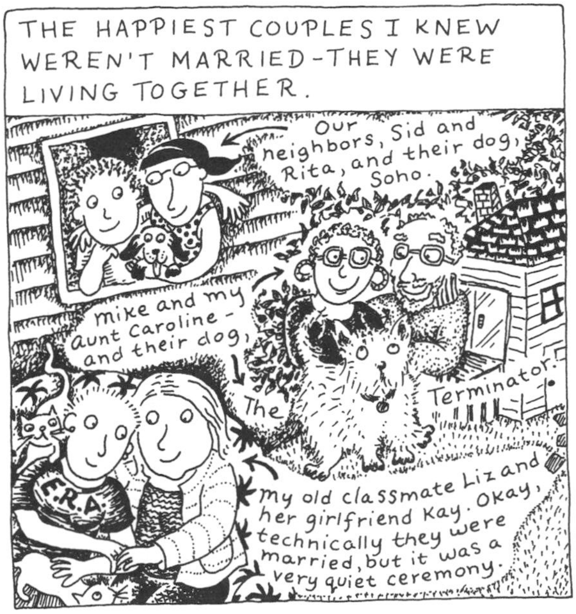
THE HAPPIEST COUPLES I KNEW WEREN'T MARRIED-THEY WERE LIVING TOGETHER.
Our neighbors, Sid and Rita, and their dog, Soho.
Mike and my aunt Caroline - and their dog,
The Terminator.
My old classmate Liz and her girlfriend Kay. Okay, technically they were married, but it was a very quiet ceremony.
E.R.A.

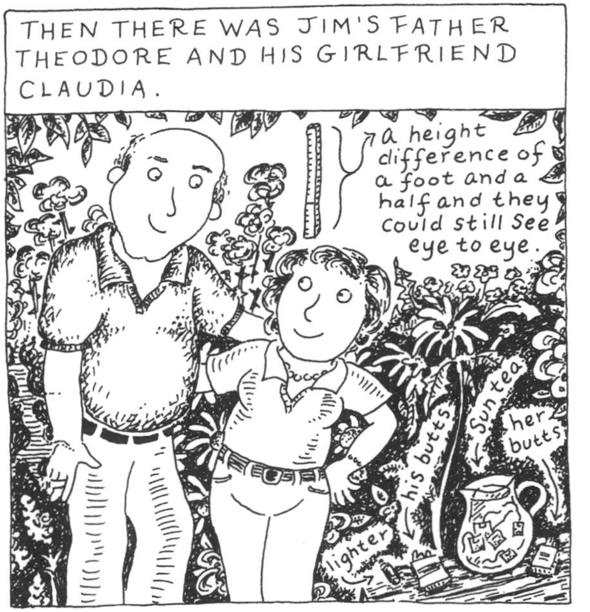
THEN THERE WAS JIM'S FATHER THEODORE AND HIS GIRLFRIEND CLAUDIA.
a height difference of a foot and a half and they could still see eye to eye.
his butts
Sun tea
her butts
lighter

THEY LIVED IN MULLBURY, NEW JERSEY, ABOUT HALF AN HOUR FROM BOSKY DELL.

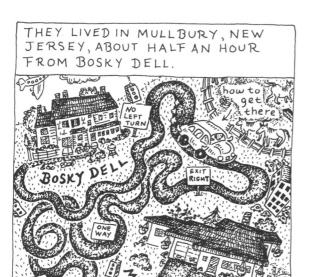

WE WENT OVER THERE FOR DINNER ALL THE TIME.

JIM'S FATHER WAS A CRANKY OLD FART WITH A HEART OF GOLD, AND I COULD NOT RESIST HIS CHARMS.

BUT WHAT I LOVED MOST ABOUT HIM WAS HOW HE LOVED HIS SON.

119

SO THIS WAS HOW A POST-BREAK-UP FATHER AND HIS GROWNUP KID COULD GET ALONG.

So Dad, do me a favor. Explain to me again how a combustion engine works.

All right, Son. Just remember, you asked for it. Now pull up a chair.

Dinner smells great.

IT HELPED THAT THEODORE HAD ACTUALLY A) MOVED OUT, B) GOTTEN A DIVORCE, AND C) FALLEN IN LOVE AGAIN WITH SOMEONE HIS OWN AGE.

CLAUDIA WAS GREAT. A DIVORCED BUSINESS MANAGER WITH THREE GROWN KIDS—WHOSE EX HAD LEFT HER FOR ANOTHER WOMAN.

How's your father?

Ucchhh...

also an uncontrollable gardener

and ridiculous Teutonic cook

SHE SMOKED MERITS, WHICH REMINDED ME OF EIGHTH GRADE.

Do you mind if I..?

Help yourself.

Mrs. Frikinmeyer is such a whore!

merits

You need a cigarette.

OR WAS JIM SO COOL WITH HIS DAD BECAUSE OF HIS BASIC SENSE OF FAIRNESS?

A HUNDRED TIMES I'D WISHED I COULD REDO THAT MOMENT WHEN DAD PUT HIS HANDS ON MY SHOULDERS.

I KNOW.

THEODORE AND CLAUDIA WERE HAPPY IN A PRICKLY SORT OF WAY, BUT HIS MOM AND FORD WERE THE HAPPIEST COUPLE I KNEW.

121

THEY WERE PROOF THAT MARRIAGE WAS A COP-OUT. JUST LOOK AT THE GRINS ON THEIR FACES AS THEY BURST THROUGH THE DOOR.

IT WAS SUNDAY, AND THEY HAD SUN ALL OVER THEM.

AND THE SUN WAS MELTING THEM TOGETHER.

WHAT?

SUDDENLY I WAS HOLDING A FISTFUL OF FUCKING DAISIES IN THE MIDDLE OF MRS. HOLDEN'S WEDDING.

AND THAT'S WHEN I BEGAN TO WANT SOMETHING DIFFERENT.

BUT I KNEW I COULDN'T HAVE IT RIGHT NOW.

Because he still can't afford to move out of his mother's house.

And because there's no point in getting married unless you want children.

Right? That's why.

SO I BOUGHT A 1974 DODGE DART SWINGER INSTEAD.

Powder blue

Price in 1986: $1,400

Swinger

P.O.S

GOD ALMIGHTY I HATED THAT CAR.

FOR ONE THING, IT HAD AN ELECTRICAL PROBLEM THEY COULD NEVER FIND.

FOR ANOTHER THING, IT LEAKED— RAIN, AND SOMETIMES ANTIFREEZE— DIRECTLY ONTO MY FEET.

BUT I REALLY HATED IT BECAUSE IT WAS MY FIRST CAR, AND WHY THE HELL SHOULD I HAVE TO DRIVE AT ALL?

JIM COULDN'T KEEP ON DRIVING ME EVERYWHERE FOREVER.

SO I CALLED TAGGART'S.

AND WITH MY NEW LICENSE I TOOK MY NEW CAR AND CRASHED IT INTO SOMEONE ELSE'S CAR.

GRUDGINGLY, AFTER THE DART WAS REPAIRED, I LEARNED THAT HAVING A CAR DIDN'T SUCK COMPLETELY.

LIKE WHEN MY MOTHER CAME OUT TO BUILD ME A SET OF BOOKSHELVES.

THEY WERE INTERLOCKING.

I WAS BEGINNING TO APPRECIATE HOW GENTLE MY MOTHER COULD BE ABOUT TELLING HER CHILDREN WHAT TO DO.

MAYBE HER FATHER WAS LIKE THAT WHEN HE WAS TEACHING HER TO MAKE THINGS OUT OF WOOD.

SHE LOVED WOOD. IT DID WHAT SHE WANTED. IT YIELDED TO HER TOUCH.

IT WAS ALSO HOW SHE GAVE US HER BLESSING.

LATELY, MAKING THINGS OUT OF WOOD HAD BECOME MY MOTHER'S WAY OF PROVIDING SUPPORT IN HER CHILDREN'S LIVES.

"OFFICE SPACE". I APPRECIATED THE WAY SHE SAID THAT. LIKE IT WASN'T ACTUALLY THE ATTIC.

MARTHA HADN'T EXACTLY FIRED ME - SHE'D GOTTEN MARRIED. AND KNOCKED UP.

SO I'D DECIDED TO START MY OWN BUSINESS, WRITING FOR MARTHA AND OTHER FREELANCE CLIENTS.

I WAS ALSO WRITING - I MEAN, SUCKING AT WRITING - A NOVEL.

AND MOM WAS OKAY WITH THIS. THAT'S WHAT THE BOOKSHELVES WERE SAYING. AND I WAS SO TOUCHED, I HAD TO ANSWER THEM.

MOM SMILED.

HER WORKSHOP. MY WORKSHOP. MY OFFICE. HER OFFICE. OH MY GOD.

I GULPED.

MOM DID NOT LOOK HAPPY WITH WHERE THIS WAS GOING.

HER PAIN WAS IN THE WOOD,
NOT IN THE WORDS.

NOW SHE DEFINITELY HAD
THAT LOOK ON HER FACE.

AND I WAS GOING TO HAVE TO
ACCEPT THAT OUR LANGUAGE
BARRIER WASN'T GOING TO CHANGE.

I HAD A DREAM THAT I RAN
INTO HIM IN A BAR.

HE TURNED OUT TO BE A VERY COOL GUY.

So you're saying, you think my mother doesn't care if I get married or not.

hic!

I COULD TALK TO HIM ABOUT ANYTHING.

With the breast cancer, I don't know if you're at higher risk because of your mom. You should just talk to your doctor.

hic!

BUT I DIDN'T KNOW WHETHER TO TAKE HIS ADVICE AFTER I WOKE UP.

Listen to the dog.

THE JOY OF SEX

I'D AVOIDED THIS SINCE MY MOTHER'S SURGERY, BUT I FINALLY HAD THE CONVERSATION WITH MY GYNO.

Yes, you are at higher risk for breast cancer because it's in your immediate family. However, there are some things you can do to lower that risk.

131

WHAT? WHAT? I'LL DO ANYTHING.

SHIT.

AND SUDDENLY I WAS HOLDING A BLANKET THAT CONTAINED MY SISTER'S SLEEPING NEWBORN BABY.

AND I WAS WONDERING: HOW THE HELL DID THIS HAPPEN?

132

I COULDN'T GET OVER THE IDEA THAT A LITTLE PIECE OF ME — EVEN IF I WAS JUST AN AUNT-HAD BEEN LET LOOSE OUT THERE.

God, I hope she doesn't end up thinking I'm an asshole...

BUT I JUST COULDN'T PICTURE HAVING A BABY MYSELF.

How about a baby with a wet nose?

diaphragm firmly inserted

IT WAS TIME FOR ANOTHER BLESSED EVENT.

IT'S A GIRL!

ONE EVENING SOON AFTER WE GOT HER, SHE SAT ON MRS. HOLDEN'S LAP IN THE KITCHEN.

Mrs. Holden favored floral caftans instead of a robe →

Tell me again why you named her Piglet.

133

SOMETHING SO BAD HAD HAPPENED THAT SHE COULDN'T MAKE DINNER. SHE COULDN'T DO ANYTHING EXCEPT SIT ON A KITCHEN CHAIR.

THE DOCTOR HAD CALLED BACK ABOUT THE BIOPSY.

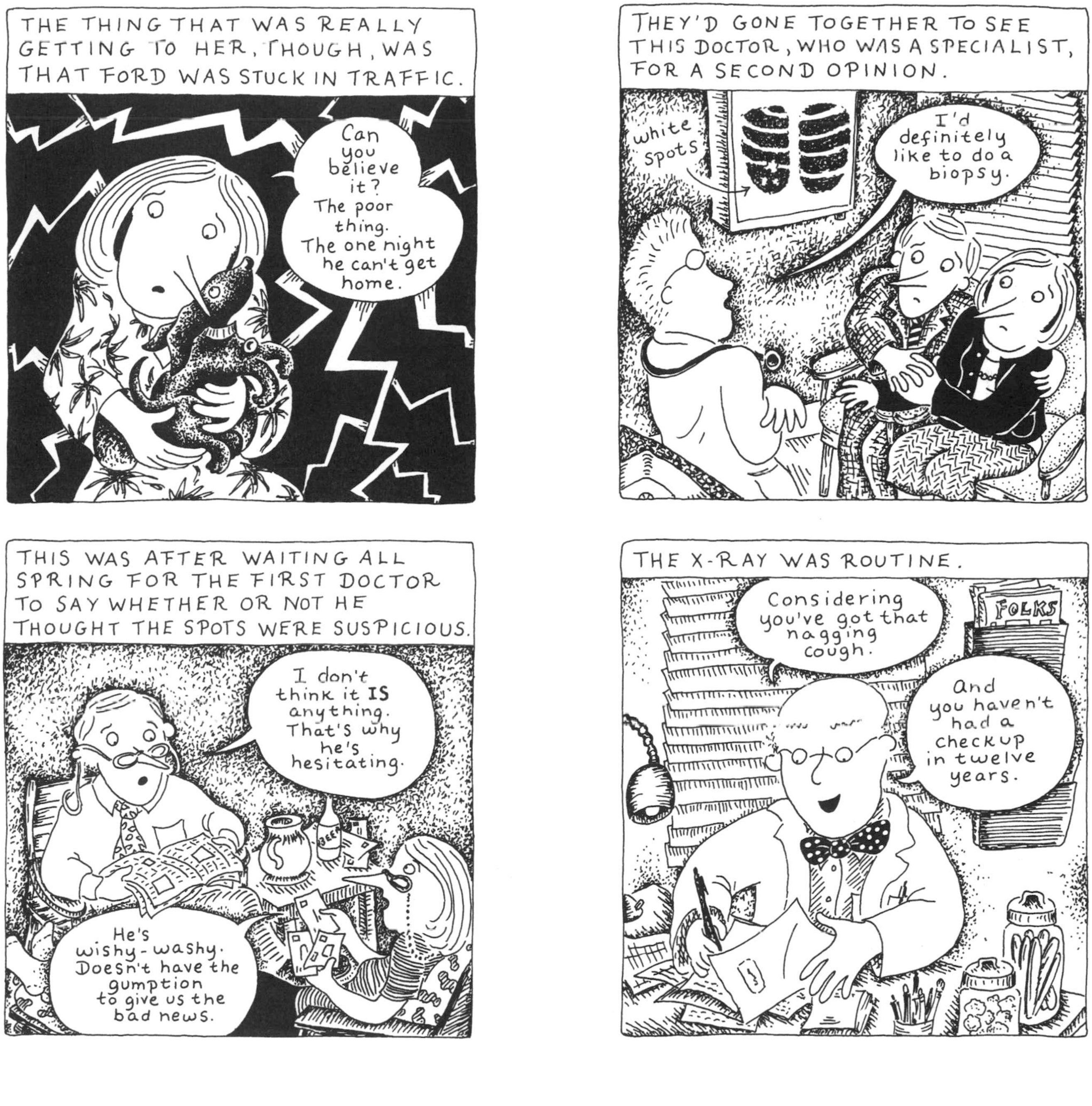
THE THING THAT WAS REALLY GETTING TO HER, THOUGH, WAS THAT FORD WAS STUCK IN TRAFFIC.
Can you believe it? The poor thing. The one night he can't get home.
THEY'D GONE TOGETHER TO SEE THIS DOCTOR, WHO WAS A SPECIALIST, FOR A SECOND OPINION.
white spots
I'd definitely like to do a biopsy.
THIS WAS AFTER WAITING ALL SPRING FOR THE FIRST DOCTOR TO SAY WHETHER OR NOT HE THOUGHT THE SPOTS WERE SUSPICIOUS.
I don't think it **IS** anything. That's why he's hesitating.
He's wishy-washy. Doesn't have the gumption to give us the bad news.
THE X-RAY WAS ROUTINE.
Considering you've got that nagging cough.
FOLKS
And you haven't had a checkup in twelve years.

SHE TOLD US ABOUT THE DIAGNOSIS THROUGH HER TEARS.

It's lung cancer.

I WAS BREATHLESS—THAT SHE COULD CRY SO PUBLICLY, AS IF SHE WERE ALONE.

Something called—

alveolar carcinoma.

THAT—TONIGHT—SHE STILL HAD THE STRENGTH TO BE SO EMOTIONALLY TRANSPARENT.

It's slow-growing, thank God. But the doctor said this kind of lung cancer is not responsive to treatment.

IT HAD ALL BEGUN WITH SUCH A SMALL SOUND. EVERY MORNING WHEN SHE MADE HER BED. FIRST THE FLOORBOARD CREAKED. THEN—

a short dry cough

AND JIM WOULD ALWAYS POKE HIS HEAD IN.

Mom, you really ought to get that checked.

MY HANDS WERE AWKWARD, AS IF THEY DIDN'T UNDERSTAND HOW THEY COULD HELP.

THE DISH FLEW INTO THE ROOM. THERE WAS NO STOPPING IT. I BEGGED IT TO BOUNCE. DON'T BREAK. JUST BOUNCE ON THE LINOLEUM FLOOR.

BUT IT BROKE. AND OUR WORLD EXPLODED INTO A MILLION PIECES.

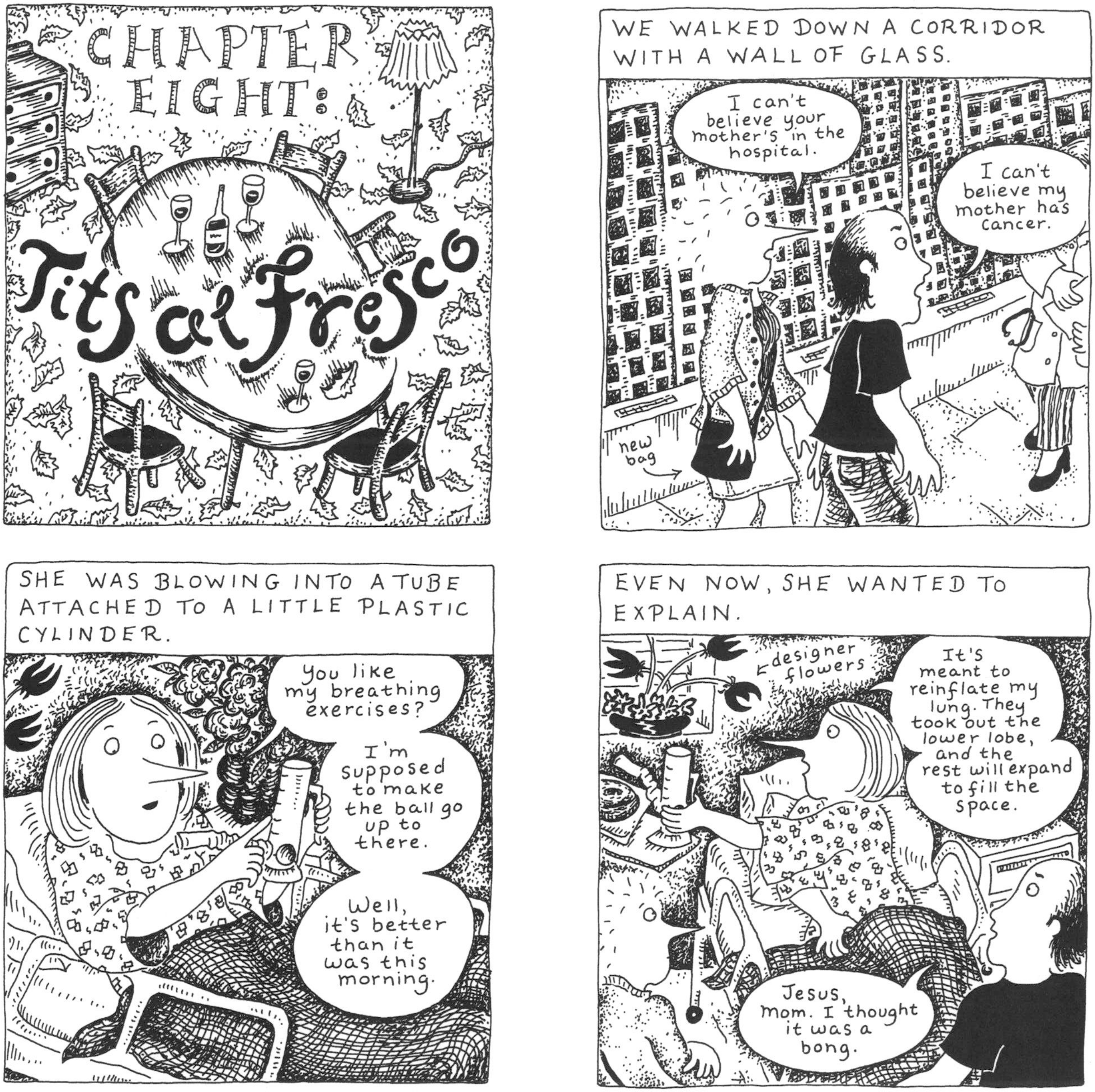
CHAPTER EIGHT:
Tits al Fresco
WE WALKED DOWN A CORRIDOR WITH A WALL OF GLASS.
I can't believe your mother's in the hospital.
I can't believe my mother has cancer.
new bag
SHE WAS BLOWING INTO A TUBE ATTACHED TO A LITTLE PLASTIC CYLINDER.
You like my breathing exercises?
I'm supposed to make the ball go up to there.
Well, it's better than it was this morning.
EVEN NOW, SHE WANTED TO EXPLAIN.
designer flowers
It's meant to reinflate my lung. They took out the lower lobe, and the rest will expand to fill the space.
Jesus, mom. I thought it was a bong.

THERE WERE NEW THINGS IN HER FACE.

THERE WERE NEW THINGS WHEN SHE CAME HOME.

FORD WORKED LESS AND STAYED HOME MORE.

JIM DIDN'T WANT TO WATCH TV.

WHENEVER I GOT UP AT NIGHT TO PEE, THERE WAS ALWAYS A LIGHT UNDER MRS. HOLDEN'S DOOR.

WHAT WAS SHE DOING IN THERE?

She isn't even sleeping.

That's because she knows she's going to die.

JESUS.

But her operation was successful.

That's what I thought.

HE SAID HE'D WALKED IN ON HER THE OTHER DAY.

140

HE'D TRIED TO COMFORT HER.

But mom, you had the surgery. I mean, they got it all, right?

SHE LOOKED DIRECTLY AT HIM. TEARS STREAMING DOWN HER FACE.

It always comes back in the other lung.

NOLI ME TANGERE.

The thing is, she never even smoked.

YET SHE BELONGED TO DEATH.

Dad, on the other hand, smokes like a chimney, drinks like a fish.

And he eats like a fucking rhinoceros.

141

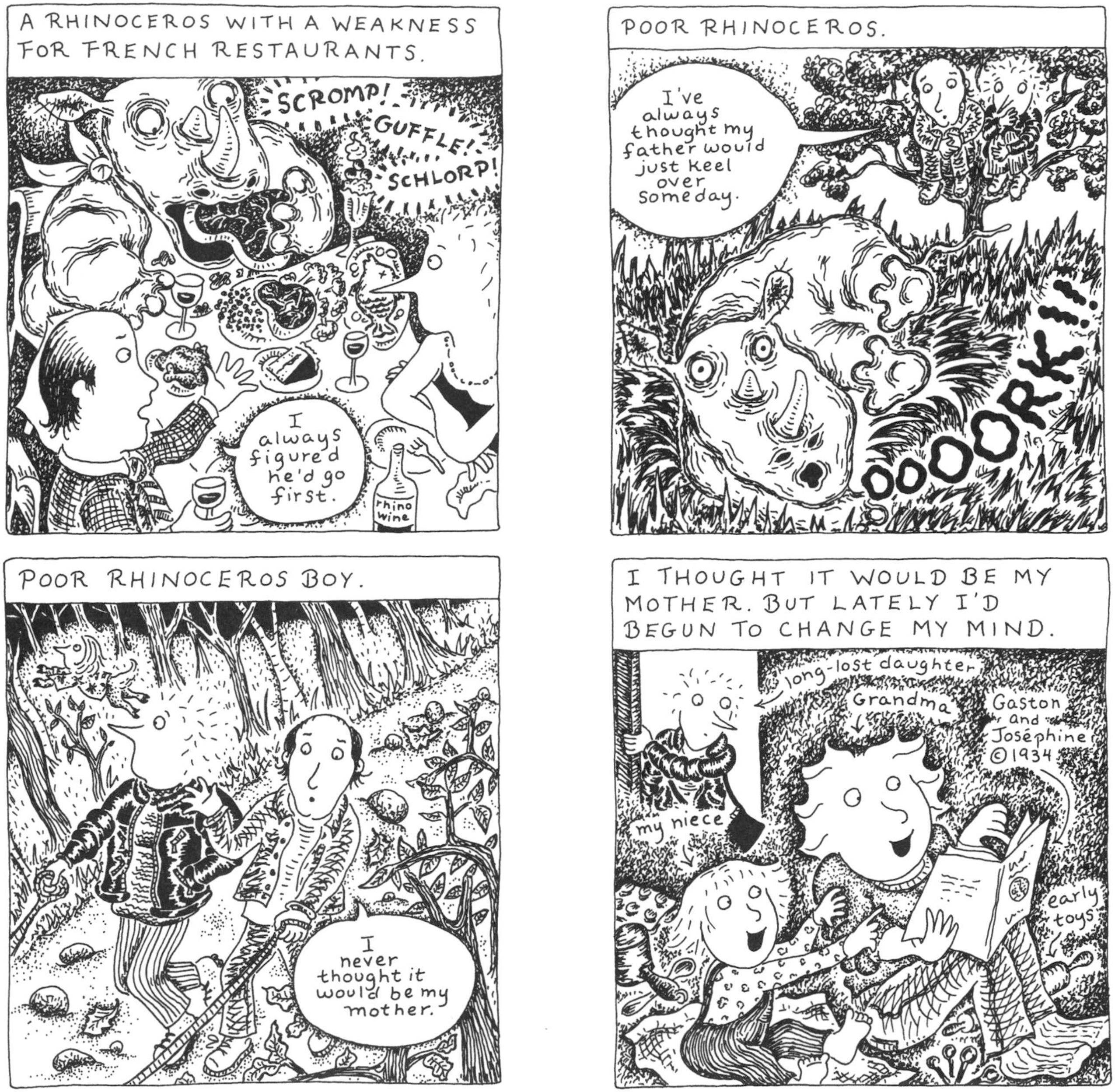
A RHINOCEROS WITH A WEAKNESS FOR FRENCH RESTAURANTS.
SCROMP!
GUFFLE!
SCHLORP!
rhino wine
I always figured he'd go first.
POOR RHINOCEROS.
I've always thought my father would just keel over someday.
OOOORK!!!
POOR RHINOCEROS BOY.
I never thought it would be my mother.
I THOUGHT IT WOULD BE MY MOTHER. BUT LATELY I'D BEGUN TO CHANGE MY MIND.
long-lost daughter
Grandma
Gaston and Joséphine ©1934
my niece
early toys

MOM HAD STARTED HER SECOND LIFE, HUSBAND OR NO HUSBAND.

THE YOUNG BLOOD OF HER FIRST GRANDCHILD POURED INTO HER VEINS, WHICH HER RELATIONSHIP WITH MY FATHER HAD SUCKED DRY.

SHE LOOKED TWENTY YEARS YOUNGER.

MEANWHILE, GRANDPA WAS GETTING HIS REVIVA-JUICE ACROSS TOWN.

AT LEAST NOW WE WERE TALKING.
Where ya been, Dad?
Oh, you know. Around.
guilt
Shopping decoy
ELEK-TRONIX HAUS
TRANSLATION:
You spent ALL DAY with Pamela! Everyone knows it!!
You've got SOME NERVE sneaking back in here and trying to be part of this family!
Yes, I was at Pamela's. It's been almost five years.
My shit with your mother might be fucked up, but Pamela and I are in a very healthy relationship.
I BEGAN TO UNDERSTAND THAT DAD HAD STARTED HIS SECOND LIFE AS WELL.
And he's just waiting for all of us to get used to it. And if we don't, we're going to lose him forever.
You have learned well, little grasshopper. And it only took you four years.
SO I GUESS, IN A WAY, I WAS READY WHEN MY BROTHER CALLED.
Dad wants us to have dinner with him and Pamela.
WHAT!?

MY BROTHER NOW WORKED FOR A PAPER IN THE CITY.

HE SAW MORE OF MY PARENTS THAN I DID, BECAUSE HE AND HIS WIFE HAD AN APARTMENT UPTOWN.

I NOTICED DAD HAD LEFT MY SISTER OUT. HE WASN'T ABOUT TO TEST HER LOYALTY TO MY MOTHER RIGHT NOW.

I COULD FEEL MY FATHER'S HANDS ON MY SHOULDERS.

145

EGGPLANT THAT LOOKED LIKE IT HAD BEEN RUN OVER BY A CAR. APPARENTLY.

THE NIGHT WAS HOT AS HELL.

SHE APOLOGIZED ABOUT THE HEAT.

SHE WAS WEARING A GAUZY PEASANT SKIRT, AND I NOTICED GLEEFULLY THAT HER HIPS HAD STARTED TO SPREAD.

YET HE WAS STILL HERE. AND HER ASS WAS DEFINITELY BIGGER. AND THEN I FOUND THE PICTURE OVER THE PIANO.

Those are my sisters. There are five of us. My poor father.

She has **FAMILY?**

THEY LOOKED SO NORMAL. NO HORNS. NO TAILS. NO HOOVES.

Are you close?

We're pretty close.

BET THEY DON'T KNOW YOU'RE DOING MY DAD.

♪ Can't you see I never **MEANT** for this to happen? ♪

I'm just a damn **FARM** GIRL! I wish I'd never come to the— ♪♪

BIG CITY! ♪♪

WHEN I STOPPED HALLUCINATING, I REALIZED THAT MAYBE THEIR RELATIONSHIP WAS MORE SERIOUS THAN I THOUGHT.

147

SHE WAS REAL. ONE HUNDRED PERCENT REAL.

Those are head shots. And those are my résumés.

grudging respect

WE LEFT THEM DOING THE DISHES LIKE AN OLD MARRIED COUPLE.

Scrub scrub

PAR OPER

OPERA SOAP

WOW.

He never did the fucking dishes for Mom.

nic fit

rat

I guess you're never too old to learn how to play house.

EVIDENTLY. BECAUSE HERE WAS "DEATH WISH" DREW, SOMEWHERE IN NEW HAMPSHIRE, FACING THE MINISTER.

NICE LITTLE BACKYARD CEREMONY. I FAILED TO ENJOY IT.

← fabric flowers still perky

(yeah, I'm lookin' at you, pal.)

I ONLY BEHAVED LIKE A LADY UNTIL WE GOT BACK IN THE CAR.

They met way after we did! He's your younger brother, for shit's sake! It should have been **US** up there!!

I BLASTED JIM FOR THREE HOURS WHILE HE DROVE US DOWN TO MASSACHUSETTS TO SPEND THE NIGHT.

Do you know how fucking sick I am of calling you my **BOYFRIEND?!**

Like, oh, we haven't been living together for seven years. He's just buying me a coke.

← wagon wheel fence ↓

His first new car, an '87 gold Honda Civic Wagon, financed by his father, thanks to a recent inheritance.

I COULDN'T BELIEVE HE DIDN'T FEEL THIS.

We basically **ARE** married.

Then what's wrong with getting up in front of everybody and saying it?

149

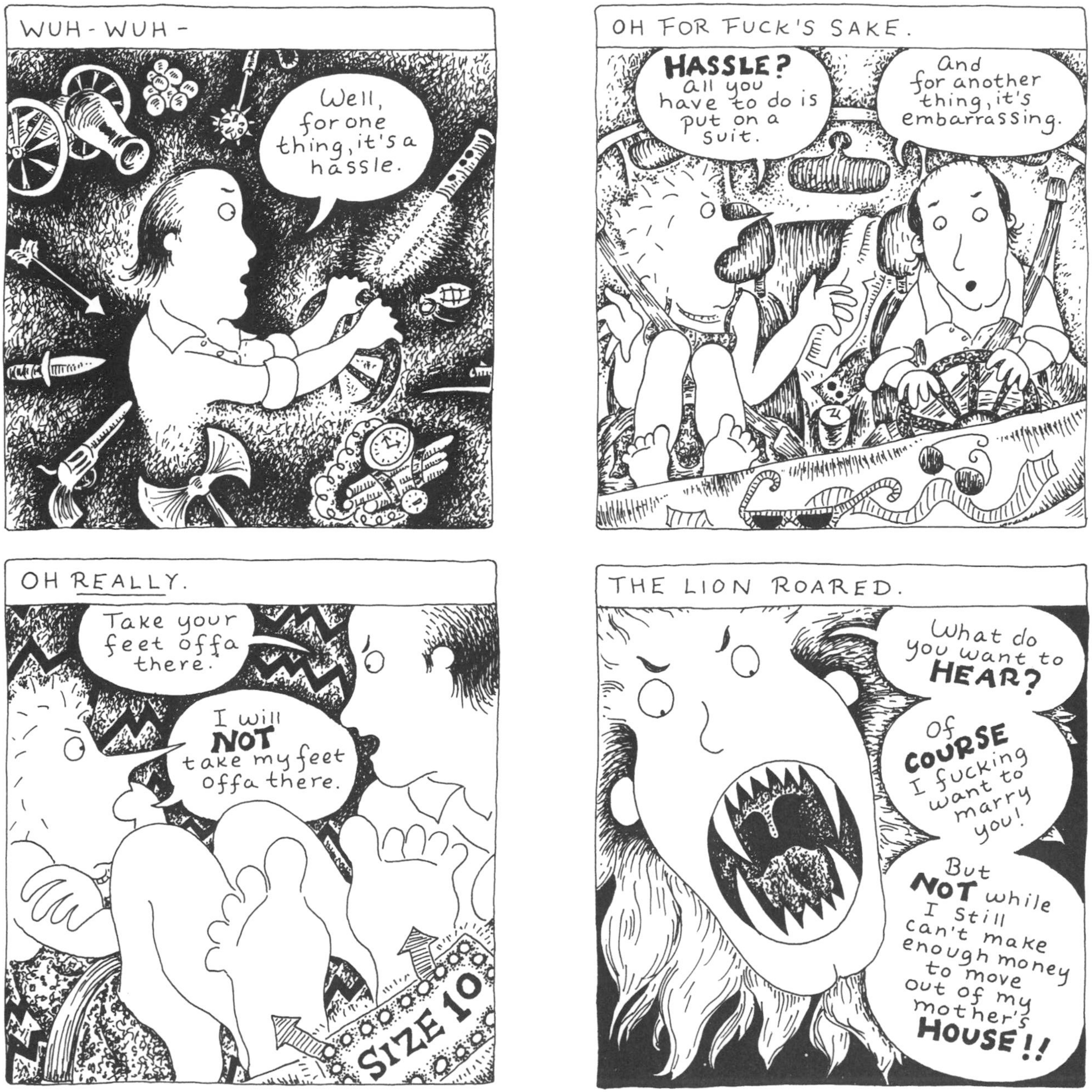
WUH-WUH-
Well, for one thing, it's a hassle.
OH FOR FUCK'S SAKE.
HASSLE? all you have to do is put on a suit.
And for another thing, it's embarrassing.
OH REALLY.
Take your feet offa there.
I will NOT take my feet offa there.
SIZE 10
THE LION ROARED.
What do you want to HEAR?
Of COURSE I fucking want to marry you!
But NOT while I still can't make enough money to move out of my mother's HOUSE!!

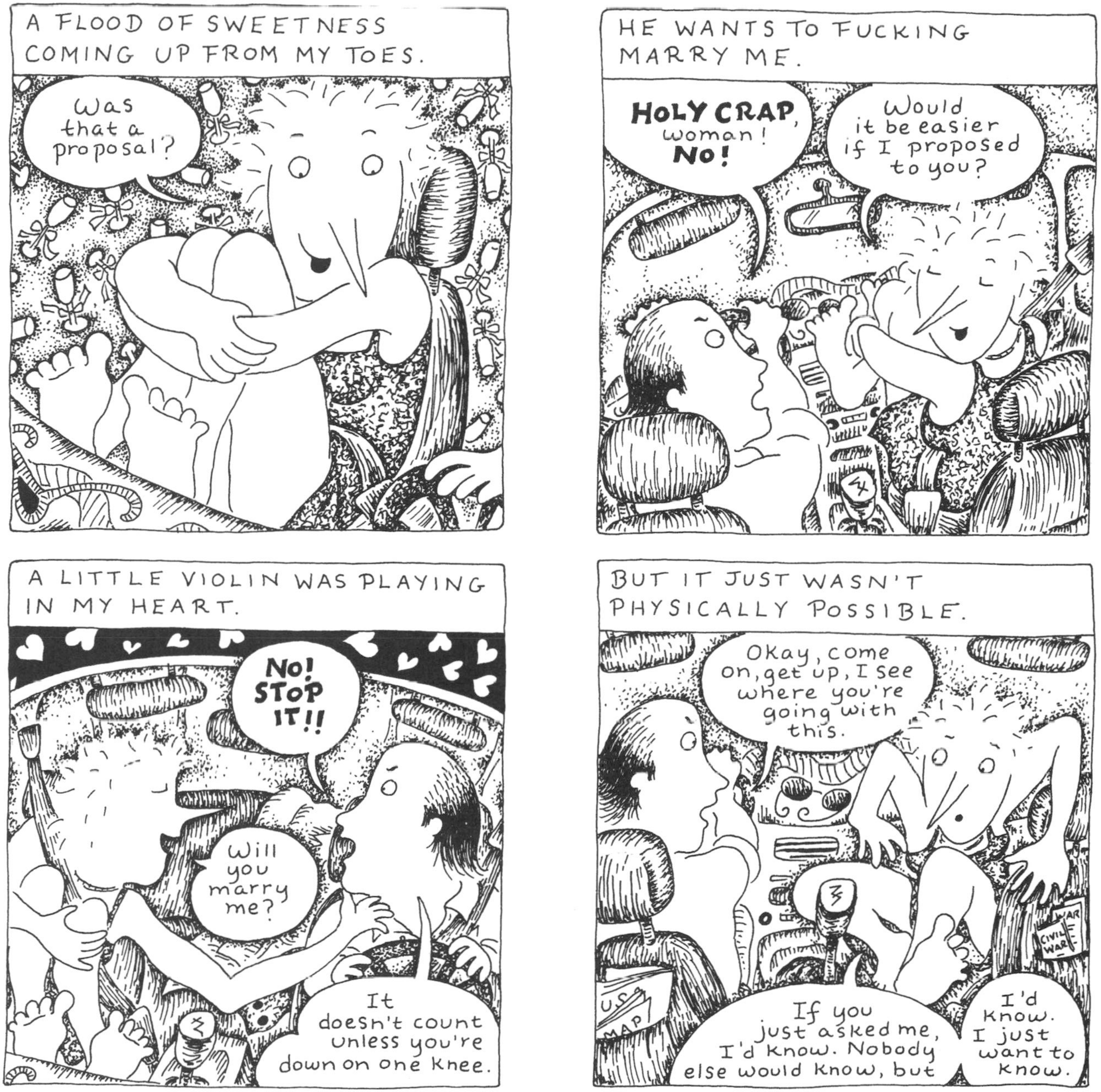

A FLOOD OF SWEETNESS COMING UP FROM MY TOES.
Was that a proposal?
HE WANTS TO FUCKING MARRY ME.
HOLY CRAP, woman! NO!
Would it be easier if I proposed to you?
A LITTLE VIOLIN WAS PLAYING IN MY HEART.
NO! STOP IT!!
Will you marry me?
It doesn't count unless you're down on one knee.
BUT IT JUST WASN'T PHYSICALLY POSSIBLE.
Okay, come on, get up, I see where you're going with this.
CIVIL WAR
U.S.A. MAP
If you just asked me, I'd know. Nobody else would know, but
I'd know. I just want to know.

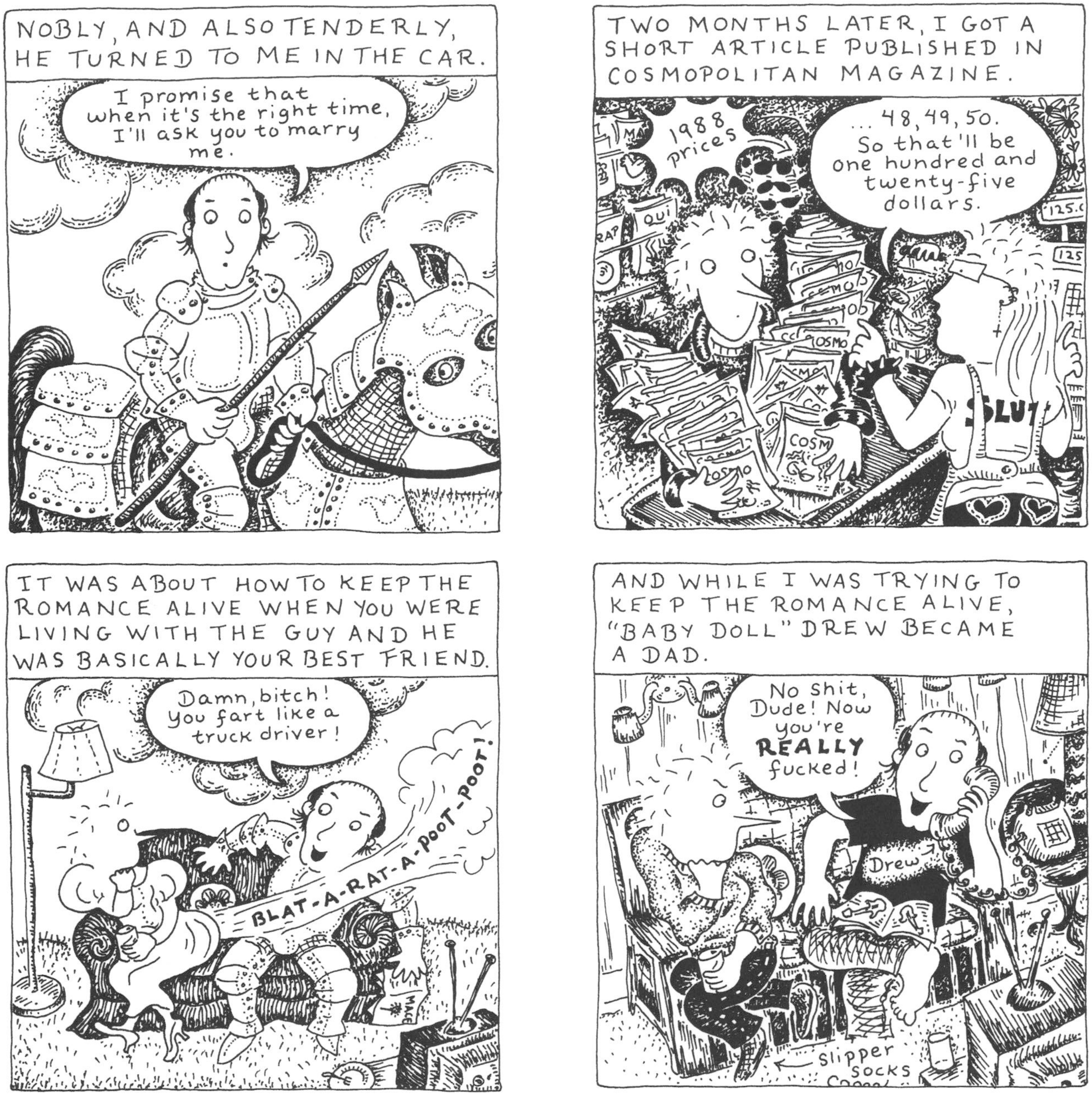
NOBLY, AND ALSO TENDERLY, HE TURNED TO ME IN THE CAR.
I promise that when it's the right time, I'll ask you to marry me.
TWO MONTHS LATER, I GOT A SHORT ARTICLE PUBLISHED IN COSMOPOLITAN MAGAZINE.
1988 prices
... 48, 49, 50. So that'll be one hundred and twenty-five dollars.
SLUT
IT WAS ABOUT HOW TO KEEP THE ROMANCE ALIVE WHEN YOU WERE LIVING WITH THE GUY AND HE WAS BASICALLY YOUR BEST FRIEND.
Damn, bitch! You fart like a truck driver!
BLAT-A-RAT-A-POOT-POOT!
AND WHILE I WAS TRYING TO KEEP THE ROMANCE ALIVE, "BABY DOLL" DREW BECAME A DAD.
No shit, Dude! Now you're **REALLY** fucked!
Drew
slipper socks

AND I FELT LIKE THIS:

OH MY GOD OH MY GOD OH MY GOD –

AND THEN I FELT SOMETHING GIVE.

We're going to be doing some travelling, and we'd like to get a little more income out of this property.

We've decided to turn the upstairs of the barn into an apartment.

If you two can afford the rent, we'd love for you to be our first tenants.

THERE WAS MORE.

If you think you might be interested, then we need your help.

We'd like to design the apartment so it really works for the two of you.

MY BONES RATTLED WITH JOY.

Oh my God. This is so unbelievable. Thank you, you guys.

Woah, Nellie. Slow down. We have no idea if we can swing this.

THE THREE OF US IGNORED HIM.

We'll leave the windows, since there are so many of them. It's too expensive to replace them all.

← mind wandering

THE PLACE FELT SO FAMILIAR. NOT BECAUSE IT WAS THE BARN, BUT BECAUSE I'D DREAMED IT.

It's the treehouse!

I HAD KNOWN THE WHAT... I JUST DIDN'T KNOW THE HOW.

Steinberger: his new axe

YEAH!

SLAM!

JIM GOT A GIG IN A WEDDING BAND.

THE BAND WAS BASED IN PHILADELPHIA.

HIS MOTHER PAID FOR IT. AND JIM'S TRANSFORMATION WAS COMPLETE.

ONE NIGHT HE ASKED ME HOW — HYPOTHETICALLY — A PERSON WAS SUPPOSED TO PROPOSE TO ANOTHER PERSON.

155

HE WAS LIKE A SWEET LITTLE WILD ANIMAL SLOWLY COMING OUT OF HIS HOLE.

NEXT THING I KNEW, WE WERE IN THE CAR, HEADED FOR VIRGINIA.

HE DID NOT PROPOSE AT DINNER.

THAT NIGHT, I DREAMED HE GAVE ME A RING.

156

THE RING WAS BEAUTIFUL. BUT I FELT SO BAD FOR HIM.

It isn't going to last. It's going to dry up and fall apart.

dusty miller

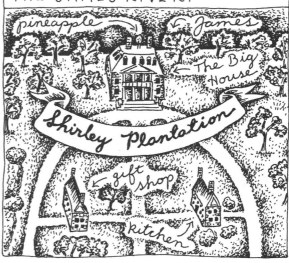

THE NEXT DAY WE TOOK A TOUR OF A PLANTATION OVERLOOKING THE JAMES RIVER.

pineapple

James

The Big House

Shirley Plantation

gift shop

kitchen

IT WAS BUILT IN 1723.

And when one of the young ladies got engaged in this room, as many of them did, she would test her diamond by seeing if it could cut glass.

THE TOUR GUIDE SHOWED US THE WINDOW.

Some o' those gals must have been real artistic.

157

I COULD FEEL JIM BEHIND ME AS WE FILED BACK OUTSIDE. THEN I HEARD HIM WHISPER IN MY EAR.

Is it time for us to announce our engagement?

I KEPT MY SHIT SO FUCKING COOL.

I don't know. Are we engaged?

I don't know. Are we?

MY SWEET LITTLE WILD ANIMAL: ALMOST ALL THE WAY OUT OF HIS HOLE.

Jim, is there something you'd like to ask me?

A question? Something you'd like to pop?

WE STOPPED AT THE EDGE OF THE RIVER.

Well, first there's something I'd like to tell you. I don't have a ring.

I know.

Okay, then, there's also a question.

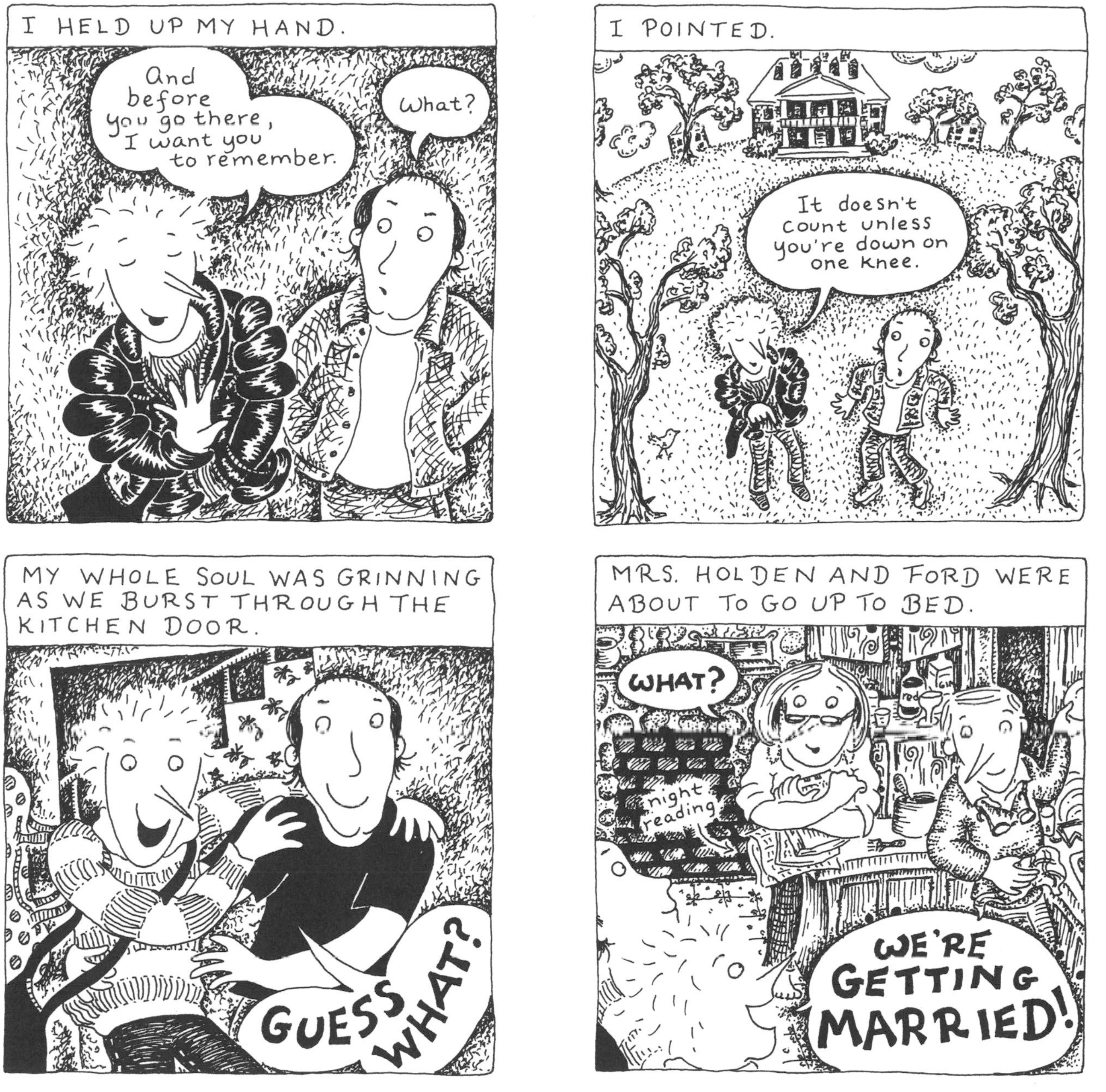
I HELD UP MY HAND.
And before you go there, I want you to remember.
What?
I POINTED.
It doesn't count unless you're down on one knee.
MY WHOLE SOUL WAS GRINNING AS WE BURST THROUGH THE KITCHEN DOOR.
GUESS WHAT?
MRS. HOLDEN AND FORD WERE ABOUT TO GO UP TO BED.
WHAT?
night reading
WE'RE GETTING MARRIED!

HER ARMS: FIRST IN THE AIR, THEN AROUND MY NECK.

HALLELUJAH!

I TOOK A DEEP BREATH.

Alice, I'm finally going to call you that, now that I'm marrying your son.

AND THAT'S HOW I MARRIED HIS MOTHER.

Oh, GOOD.

AND THIS IS HOW I MARRIED HIS FATHER.

Two years ago, my sister died. My mother had left her engagement and wedding ring set to her when she died, which my sister never used. She left the rings to Jim.

Why didn't you tell me?

HE WAS SILENT.
Jim sold the rings back to me for a car.
Ow!
Punch!
SO THAT'S HOW HE GOT THE HONDA CIVIC WAGON. SCHMUCK.
Feel free to reset the stones if you think the old settings are ugly.
velvet box he pulled out of his pocket
I OPENED THE BOX AND SAW THE MOST HEART-STOPPINGLY BEAUTIFUL RINGS EVER MADE.
Oh my God, they're gorgeous!
Small "European-cut" diamond in vintage platinum setting
vintage matching wedding band with diamond chips
BUT THEY WEREN'T JIM'S, WERE THEY?
Well, Theodore, I guess this means you and I are finally tying the knot.

HE GAVE THE RINGS TO JIM, WHO GAVE THE ENGAGEMENT RING TO ME.

MY NEW DIAMOND THREW RAINBOWS ACROSS THE WALLS.

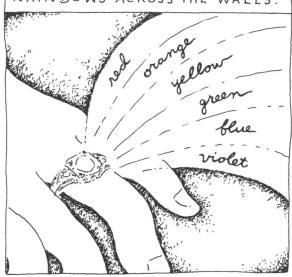

I WAS INSIDE THE RAINBOW. I WAS A HOSTESS IN A YELLOW DRESS.

A YELLOW DRESS, AND I'D BE SO LOVED, AND THE UNIVERSE WOULD BE SHINY WITH JOY.

BUT THERE WAS NO YELLOW DRESS.

It's back.

ONLY ALICE'S WHITE, WHITE FACE.

They found a spot on the other lung.

HER WHITE FACE ON THAT BLACK, BLACK NIGHT.

Can't they operate?

There's no point.

GOD **DAMMIT**, WOMAN!

What do you mean, there's no point?

Nothing works on this stuff. Radiation, chemo, surgery. I won't put myself through it.

JIM KEPT IT TOGETHER.

So what are you going to do?

SHE HAD THE LOOK OF SOMEONE WHO HAS MISSED THE LAST TRAIN AND IS FORCING HER FOOTSTEPS BACK TO THE EMPTY STATION.

Hospice.

When it's time.

JIM SHOOK HIS HEAD.

Well, one thing's for sure, mom. You've got balls.

AND I THOUGHT ABOUT BOTH OF THEIR BALLS.

HIS

HERS

wow.

NOW SHE TOOK HALCYON TO SLEEP, BUT THE PAIN WAS STILL OUTSIDE HER DOOR.

WAITING.

How much time does she have?

Some people with this die in six months. Some people make it a couple of years.

I QUESTIONED MY MOTIVES, BUT IT SEEMED TO ME WE SHOULDN'T LEAVE THE WEDDING AS PLANNED—TILL NEXT MAY.

I think we should move it up.

TO MY AMAZEMENT, HE AGREED.

My mother said the same thing.

165

SHE WAS BRINGING MY WEDDING CLOSER, EVEN AS SHE WAS MOVING AWAY.

AND SPEAKING OF MOVING AWAY.

IT DIDN'T SEEM VERY FAST TO ME.

UNTIL THEY INSTALLED THE SHOWER/TUB.

THEN IT HIT ME.

We're going to live here. Alone.

WE'D ALWAYS LIVED WITH OTHER PEOPLE. IN THE DORM. IN PHILLY AND BOSKY DELL, WITH ALICE AND FORD.

What if we don't get along?

WHAT IF THE ONLY THING THAT HELD US TOGETHER WAS OUR HATRED OF THE COMMON ENEMY?

Well, not hatred. But you know what I mean. minor irritation.

What, because you've only been with him for eight years?

SUDDENLY IT SEEMED LIKE WE WERE BEING RASH.

Rash. Yeah, that was the word I was looking for.

Well, what if we don't know each other that well?

What if we only think we do?

167

I FELT A COLD BREEZE PASSING OVER MY FEET.

YES, THAT'S ALL, I THOUGHT, LOOKING AT THE BARE BOARDS OF OUR NEW PLACE IN THE WORLD.

ENOUGH LOVE, MAYBE, BUT DEFINITELY NOT ENOUGH TIME. NOW THAT WE HAD TO FAST-TRACK THE WEDDING.

THERE WAS SO MUCH I HAD NEVER THOUGHT ABOUT. NOW IT WAS ALL I WAS SUPPOSED TO THINK ABOUT.

168

NATURALLY, MY BRAIN EXPLODED.

I LEARNED THAT PLANNING A WEDDING WAS THE TOTAL OPPOSITE OF HAVING ONE.

OR MAYBE IT WAS THE BEGINNING OF THE MARRIAGE.

HE'D HAD IT SINCE FOURTH GRADE.

SINCE THE WEDDING WAS GOING TO BE AT THE HOUSE IN BOSKY DELL, ALICE HELPED WITH THE PLANNING TOO. MY MOM CAME OUT FOR A VISIT.

ALICE WAS ALREADY GETTING READY FOR THE MEETING WITH THE CATERER, ON THE PORCH.

AS WE CAME IN, THEY HUGGED.

AND IT SEEMED TO ME THAT THEY BECAME ONE PERSON.

THE WOMAN WHO RAISED ME...

AND THE WOMAN WHO DID ALL THE TALKING...

MERGED. AND I FELT WRAPPED IN THEIR EXPERIENCE.

AND JIM BROUGHT HIS CLIPBOARD.

Okay. So for hors d'oeuvres we'll do the gravlax, the egg rolls, **AND** the scallops.

I mean, we don't want to starve.

AUGUST: THE LAST NAIL WENT INTO THE BARN APARTMENT, AND WE STOOD ON THE THRESHOLD OF OUR NEW LIFE.

Wow! All it needs is a coat of paint!

the threshold of our new bedroom, as a matter of fact.

171

FORD SMILED.

WE FROZE AS THE TRAP WAS SPRUNG.

THERE WAS A RINGING IN MY EARS.

I WAS WONDERING WHAT ALL THAT SHIT WAS.

BUT WE GOT THE HANG OF IT. JIM ROLLED THE WALLS IN THE AFTERNOONS, AND I WAS THE MICHELANGELO OF TRIM.

I FOUND PAINTING VERY ZEN, LIKE DRAWING WHEN I WAS YOUNG. PART OF MY MIND WENT TO SLEEP, AND ANOTHER PART WOKE UP.

I HEARD A LITTLE CHILD.

IT WAS RUNNING THROUGH THE BLINDING SUNLIGHT, DISAPPEARING DOWN THE HALL.

173

AND I REALIZED IT WAS OURS.

SEVENTEEN CANS OF LATEX LATER, JIM AND I STARTED CARRYING FURNITURE ACROSS THE LAWN.

SID AND RITA GAVE US A TABLE AND CHAIRS.

I BOUGHT A SET OF PICNIC UTENSILS WITH BLUE PLASTIC HANDLES.

THEY WERE THE COLOR OF THE END OF THE DAY.

WHEN I WAS ABOUT TO TAKE MY FIRST SHOWER, I REALIZED I DIDN'T NEED TO PUT ON A ROBE.

FOR THE FIRST TIME IN MY TWENTY-EIGHT YEARS, I FINALLY WASN'T LIVING WITH A SHITLOAD OF OTHER PEOPLE.

I DIDN'T WALK TO THE BATHROOM. I DANCED.

175

THEN IT WAS TIME.

MY FATHER WAS WAITING AT THE BOTTOM OF THE STAIRS.

I TOOK HIS ARM AND SMILED.

WE GATHER HERE TODAY TO CELEBRATE THE ANCIENT AND HOLY RITUAL OF MARRIAGE.

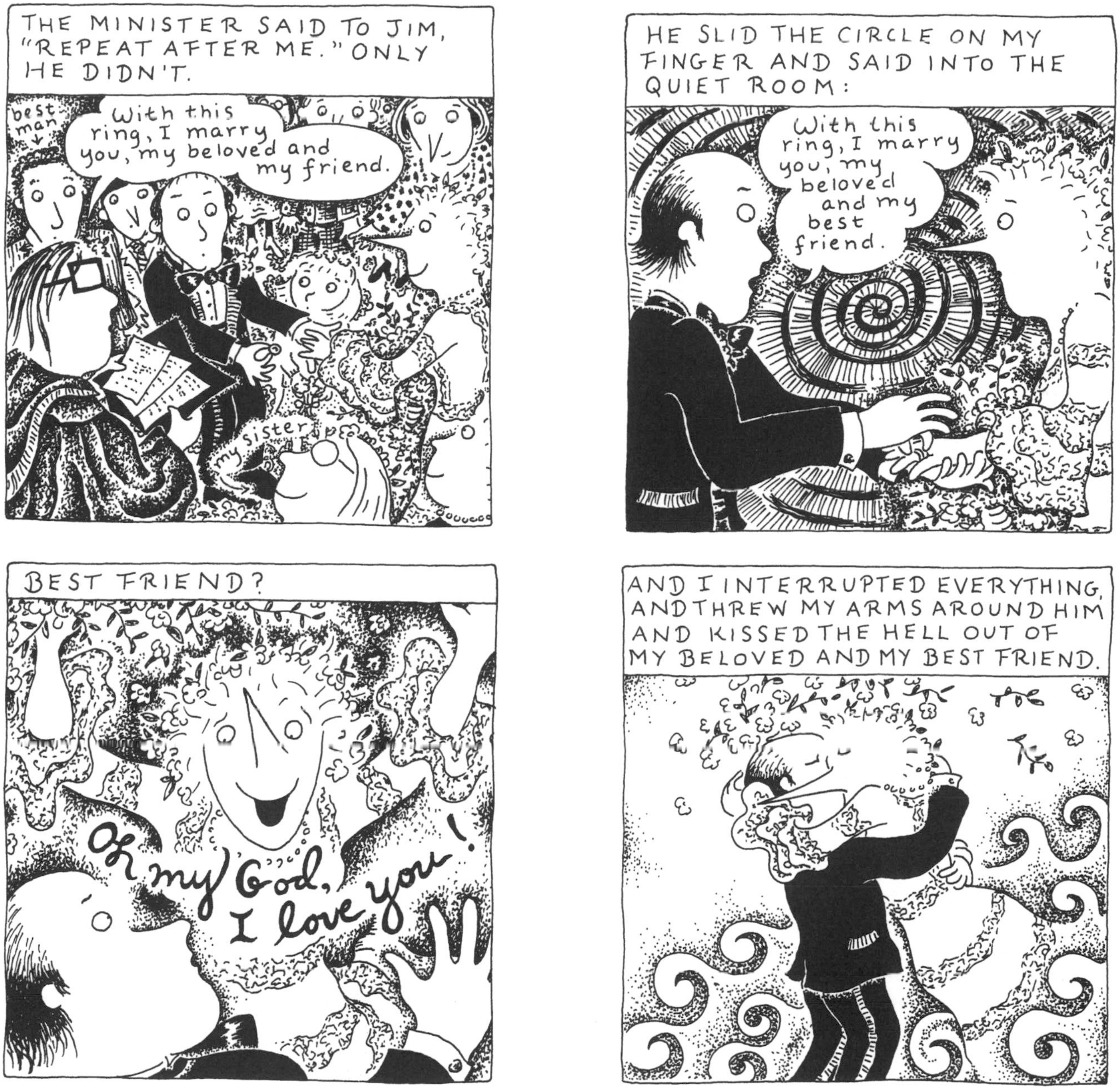
THE MINISTER SAID TO JIM, "REPEAT AFTER ME." ONLY HE DIDN'T.
best man
With this ring, I marry you, my beloved and my friend.
my sister
HE SLID THE CIRCLE ON MY FINGER AND SAID INTO THE QUIET ROOM:
With this ring, I marry you, my beloved and my best friend.
BEST FRIEND?
Oh my God, I love you!
AND I INTERRUPTED EVERYTHING, AND THREW MY ARMS AROUND HIM AND KISSED THE HELL OUT OF MY BELOVED AND MY BEST FRIEND.

CHAPTER NINE: TENDER TITS

WE MADE A HUGE BANNER OF BIRTHDAY MESSAGES OUT OF AN OLD SHEET, WHICH WE ALL WROTE AND DREW ON.

HERE'S WHAT WE DIDN'T WRITE:

178

EVEN THOUGH THAT'S WHAT WE ALL WERE THINKING.

SHE HAD RISEN.

EXACTLY.

OKAY.

179

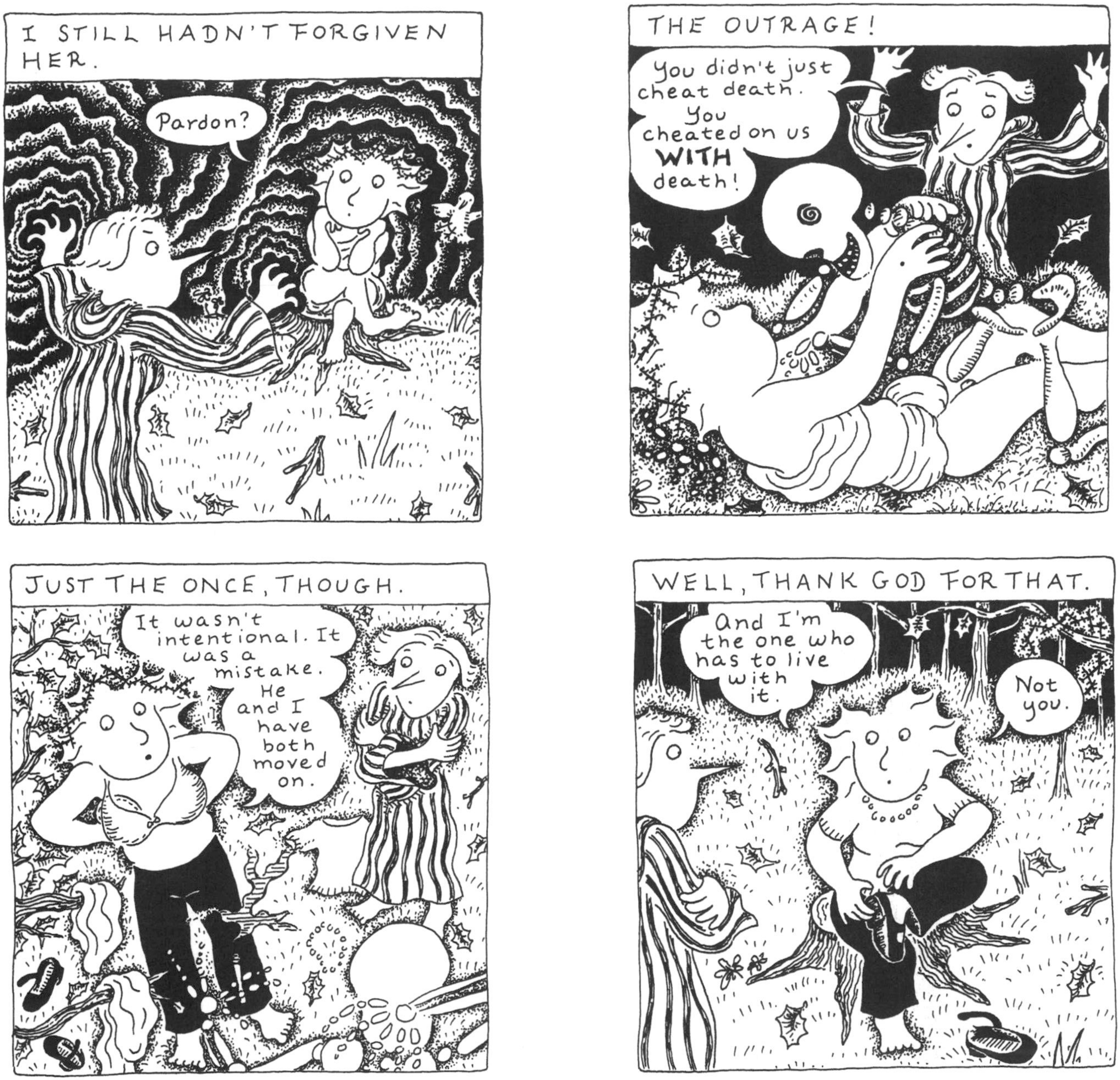
I STILL HADN'T FORGIVEN HER.
Pardon?
THE OUTRAGE!
You didn't just cheat death. You cheated on us **WITH** death!
JUST THE ONCE, THOUGH.
It wasn't intentional. It was a mistake. He and I have both moved on.
WELL, THANK GOD FOR THAT.
And I'm the one who has to live with it.
Not you.

SHE WAS INFURIATINGLY CALM.

"LIVE."

THE ONE WHO WASN'T LIVING WAS MY FATHER.

CHRISTMAS. I WAS DRIVING MY CAR A FEW DAYS LATER WHEN TEARS SUDDENLY STARTED RUNNING DOWN MY FACE.

WHAT AM I, I THOUGHT, TEN YEARS OLD?

WE'D BEEN SITTING AROUND THE DAY AFTER CHRISTMAS WHEN HE CAME IN TO SAY GOODBYE.

I'm afraid it's time for me to go.

MOM WAS IN THE KITCHEN.

I don't know if your mother told you.

I'm moving to upstate New York.

SHE DIDN'T HAVE TO TELL US.

What are these pictures?

Dad and Pamela bought a farmhouse. They've been looking for a while.

I ASKED HER HOW SHE KNEW.

MY BROTHER LOOKED AT ME.

I WAS STILL SURPRISED AND DRY-EYED WHEN I KISSED HIS CHEEK GOODBYE.

BUT A FEW DAYS LATER, IT STARTED TO FEEL LIKE THIS:

ALTHOUGH I WAS, IN FACT, THIRTY FUCKING YEARS OLD.

OLD ENOUGH TO BE ON MY WAY TO MY FIRST MAMMOGRAM.

THANKS TO MY GYNO.

THE TECHNICIAN HOISTED MY BREAST ONTO THE FREEZING MACHINE, AND SQUEEZED THE SHIT OUT OF IT UNDER A PIECE OF GLASS.

THEN SHE CRUSHED THE FUCK OUT OF THE OTHER ONE.

AT LEAST I DIDN'T HAVE TO START GETTING REGULAR MAMMOGRAMS TILL I WAS THIRTY-FIVE.

TIME WAS PASSING MORE DISTINCTLY. AND I WAS SURPRISED TO FIND THAT MY EDGES WERE SOFTENING.

I WAS FEELING DIPPED IN SOME SORT OF RIVER OF ONGOING WOMANHOOD.

185

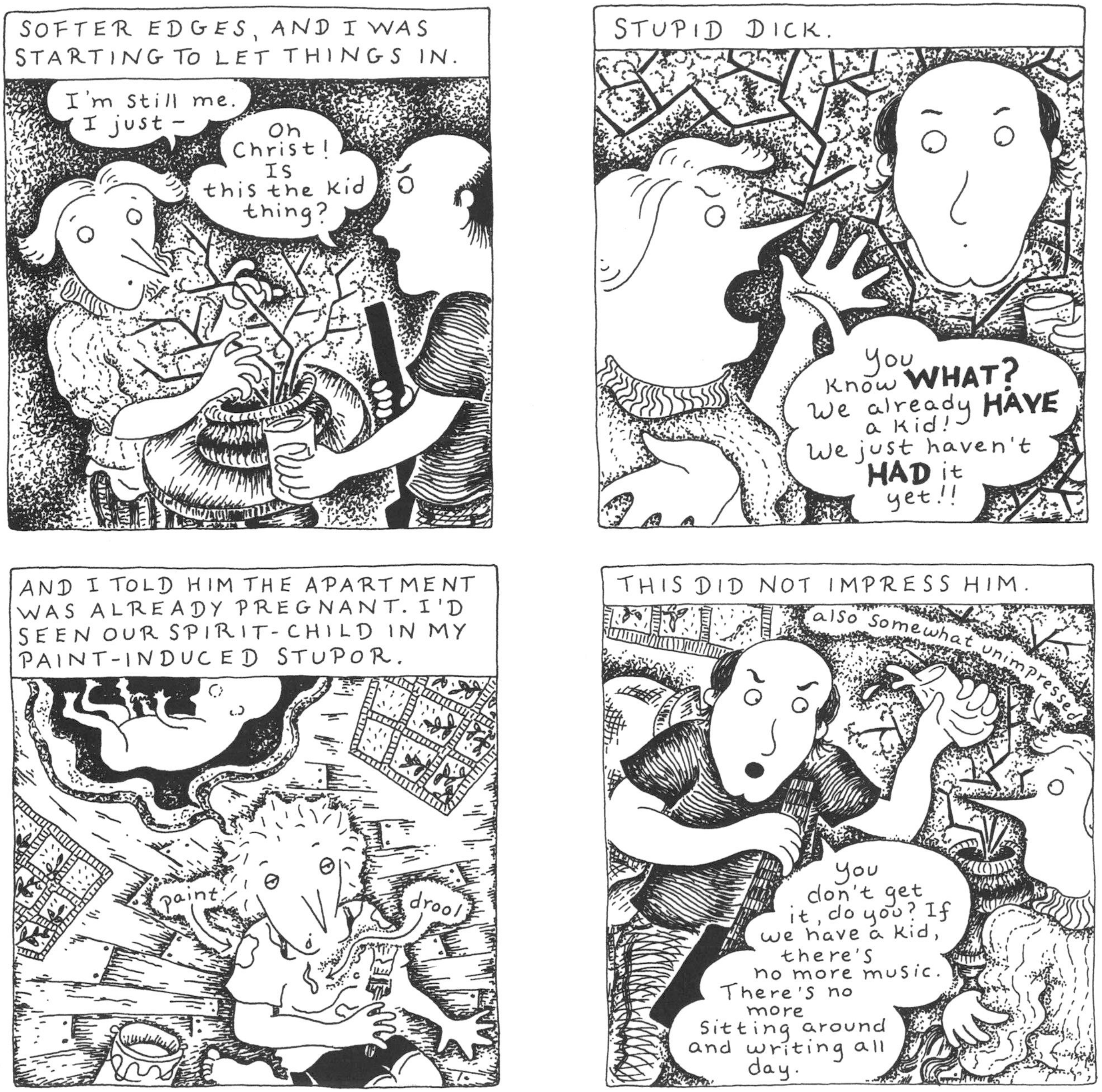
SOFTER EDGES, AND I WAS STARTING TO LET THINGS IN.
I'm still me. I just -
Oh Christ! Is this the kid thing?
STUPID DICK.
You know **WHAT?** We already **HAVE** a kid! We just haven't **HAD** it yet!!
AND I TOLD HIM THE APARTMENT WAS ALREADY PREGNANT. I'D SEEN OUR SPIRIT-CHILD IN MY PAINT-INDUCED STUPOR.
paint
drool
THIS DID NOT IMPRESS HIM.
also somewhat unimpressed
You don't get it, do you? If we have a kid, there's no more music. There's no more sitting around and writing all day.

NOW, IN ADDITION TO PLAYING WEDDINGS ALL WEEKEND AND GIVING LESSONS, HE WAS ALSO COMPOSING HIS OWN MUSIC.

Look, I'm the one who really stands to lose, here. I'm the one who has to carry it. And give birth to it. I'm the one who has to nurse it. And I have to give up my writing room, so you can keep teaching in your studio.

I'D KNOWN IT WOULD BE THE NURSERY FROM THE DAY I MOVED IN.

ⓐ windows facing south, awash in happy baby light...

God dammit.

heavy as shit Toshiba laptop.

ⓑ one low window a toddler can see out of.

new rug

my sister's old futon, for overnight guests—platform made by mom

Books

ⓒ it's also the furthest room from the stairs...

JIM GOT SNARLY.

And where's the money going to come from?

the teeth don't scare me now

Hand-me-downs. Yard sales. The kid doesn't care what it has. Not in the beginning.

LION TIME:

You know, a baby isn't like a new bag. You don't just get one because everybody else has one.

Is that why you're so hell-bent on this?

COOL. BE COOL.

FUCK!

HE WAS RIGHT, THOUGH. WE WERE GETTING OUR MARRIAGE LICENSE WHEN I KNEW.

Clerk of Bosky Dell

Martha, our witness. Knocked up again.

No, you don't want that. That's a dog license.

I'D SUDDENLY REALIZED THERE WAS MORE TO THIS MARRIAGE THING AFTER ALL.

I SLUMPED INTO A CHAIR.

Look. I get it. We both like to do our thing. Our life is based on that.

But here's my question.

slump!

188

I WAS STARING LIMPLY INTO SPACE.

What if we spend our lives doing this, seeing if we've got something to offer and find out, in the end, that we're not as good as we thought?

That the one lasting good thing we could've done was raise a kid?

And we didn't?

SLUMP!

OOF!

WE STARED AT EACH OTHER IN SHOCK THROUGH THE QUESTIONABLE FLOWERS.

MEANWHILE, JIM'S BROTHER DREW, THE DOLL-SLAYER, AND HIS WIFE GAVE BIRTH TO BABY NUMBER TWO.

Two rugrats! Nightmare!

...Yeah, I'm getting a certain amount of heat about it from the old ball-and-chain...

AND MY BIGGEST CLIENT WAS TURNING INTO A BALLOON.

SO I'D FOUND A JOB WITH A SMALL COMPANY, WRITING MARKETING COMMUNICATIONS.

SIX MONTHS LATER, SHE SAID SHE HAD AN ANNOUNCEMENT TO MAKE.

MY FIRST REACTION WAS:

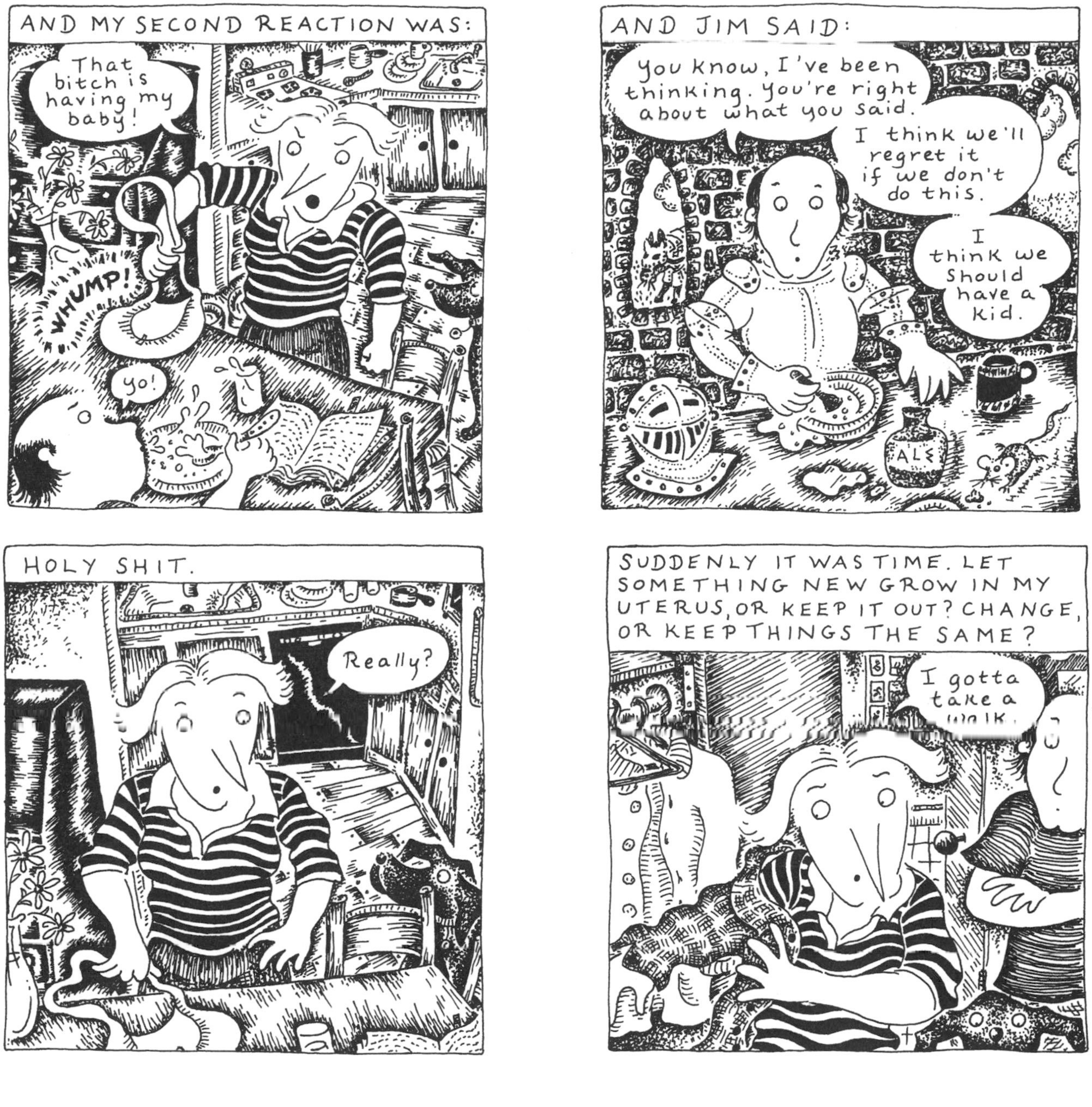
AND MY SECOND REACTION WAS:
That bitch is having my baby!
WHUMP!
Yo!
AND JIM SAID:
You know, I've been thinking. You're right about what you said.
I think we'll regret it if we don't do this.
I think we should have a kid.
ALE
HOLY SHIT.
Really?
SUDDENLY IT WAS TIME. LET SOMETHING NEW GROW IN MY UTERUS, OR KEEP IT OUT? CHANGE, OR KEEP THINGS THE SAME?
I gotta take a walk.

I WENT TO MY FAVORITE THINKING PLACE, THE OLD LOCK ON THE CANAL, AND WATCHED THE WATER BOIL BELOW THE SLUICE.

LIFE IS LIKE A LOVER, THE WATER SEEMED TO BE SAYING.

YOU HAVE TO SURRENDER YOURSELF COMPLETELY TO IT IF YOU WANT TO GET ANYTHING OUT OF IT.

TURNED OUT IT WAS HARDER TO GIVE UP THE BIRTH CONTROL THAN I THOUGHT.

AND THEN THERE WAS ANOTHER KIND OF SURRENDER... AS THE RHINOCEROS, WITH A TERRIBLE HEAVE, FELL ONTO THE GRASS.

HE SUFFERED A MASSIVE HEART ATTACK AND WAS DEAD BEFORE HE REACHED THE GROUND.

ON A BEAUTIFUL SUNDAY. AFTER A MORNING OF YARDWORK. WITH TWO BAGS OF GRASS CLIPPINGS IN HIS HANDS.

CLAUDIA CALLED. SHE TOLD US TO MEET HER AT THE HOSPITAL. THE EMT'S WERE STILL WORKING ON HIM IN THE AMBULANCE.

THEY HAD TO—TILL THE EMERGENCY ROOM DOCTOR COULD PRONOUNCE HIM DEAD.

THE FOUR OF US WATCHED THROUGH THE WINDOW.

THIS WAS BEFORE CELL PHONES, SO WE COULDN'T REACH JIM, WHO WAS PLAYING TWO GIGS THAT DAY OUTSIDE PHILADELPHIA.

CLAUDIA CAME RUNNING IN, HER NEW CHEMO WIG SLIGHTLY ASKEW.

SHE'D BEEN DIAGNOSED WITH BREAST CANCER AND WAS RECEIVING TREATMENT FOLLOWING HER MASTECTOMY.

SHE IDENTIFIED THE BODY.

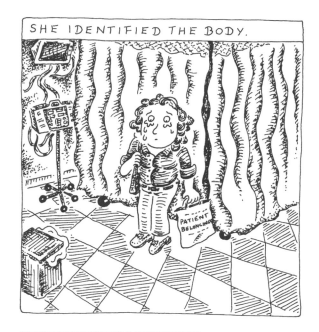

THEN WE WENT IN TO SAY GOODBYE. THEODORE WAS THE FIRST DEAD PERSON I'D EVER SEEN IN MY LIFE.

WAY UNDER HIS SKIN, A BLUISH LAVENDER COLOR WAS SPREADING ALL OVER HIM LIKE A BRUISE.

CLAUDIA STAYED TO FILL OUT PAPERWORK, WHILE WE CRIED IN THE PARKING LOT.

THEN I DID THE THIRD WORST THING I EVER HAD TO DO. *

* I had to do it; it was inescapable; but it still felt terrible.

I WAITED UP FOR JIM, AND WHEN HE CAME HOME I TOLD HIM HIS FATHER WAS DEAD.

NIGHT PASSED OVER US AS WE LAY NEXT TO EACH OTHER, TALKING, TRYING TO GRASP THE EDGES OF A CHANGED WORLD.

FEELING THE TIES THAT HAD ONCE BOUND US TO HIM FLYING FREE, BEGGING FOR SOMEONE TO CATCH ONTO.

TOUCHING THE EDGES OF A GAPING HOLE.

AND THOUGH I WAS LYING NEXT TO HIM, I COULD HARDLY IMAGINE WHAT JIM FELT. IT WASN'T MY DAD.

NIGHT PASSED. DAY CAME. BUT IT WAS STILL NIGHT.

AND NIGHT QUESTIONS - THE KIND YOU CAN'T ANSWER - FILLED THE DAY.

THE ONLY THING THAT WASN'T A QUESTION WAS PLANNING THEODORE'S FUNERAL.

CLAUDIA INCLUDED THE BOYS IN ALL THE ARRANGEMENTS, AND I WENT WITH JIM FOR SUPPORT.

WE BURIED THEODORE IN A BEAUTIFUL CEMETERY OUTSIDE BOSTON, IN THE SAME SUBURB WHERE HE'D GROWN UP.

RIGHT NEXT TO HIS MOTHER, HIS FATHER, AND HIS SISTER!

HE'D ASKED TO BE BURIED IN THE FAMILY PLOT. WE WONDERED HOW HE'D FEEL ABOUT SPENDING ETERNITY WITH THEM.

DREW AND HIS WIFE DROVE DOWN FROM NEW HAMPSHIRE, LEAVING THE RUGRATS AT HOME.

WE GOT HAMMERED.

199

A FEW YEARS LATER, CLAUDIA'S TREATMENTS STOPPED WORKING AND SHE DIED OF BREAST CANCER.

THE HOUSE SHE'D SHARED WITH THEODORE IN MULLBURY WENT TO HER CHILDREN, WHO SOLD IT.

THE ROAD THAT LED TO THE HOUSE WAS CLOSED AND REROUTED, REMOVING EVEN OUR ACCESS TO THEIR VANISHED WORLD.

EVERYTHING ABOUT GOING OVER THERE FOR DINNER WAS GONE.

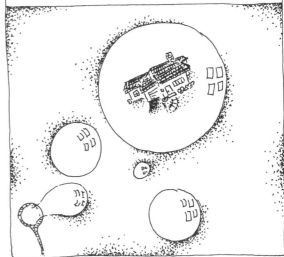

LEAVING ONLY BOOKCASES, A BUREAU, SOME TABLES AND CHAIRS.

THREE MONTHS LATER. ME AND MY DAD. NOT SAYING MUCH. WALKING AROUND HIS NEW PLACE.

JIM AND I HAD FINALLY GONE UP THERE, TO CELEBRATE MY DAD'S SIXTY-FIFTH BIRTHDAY.

...AFTER JIM CONVINCED ME TO ACCEPT PAMELA'S INVITATION.

201

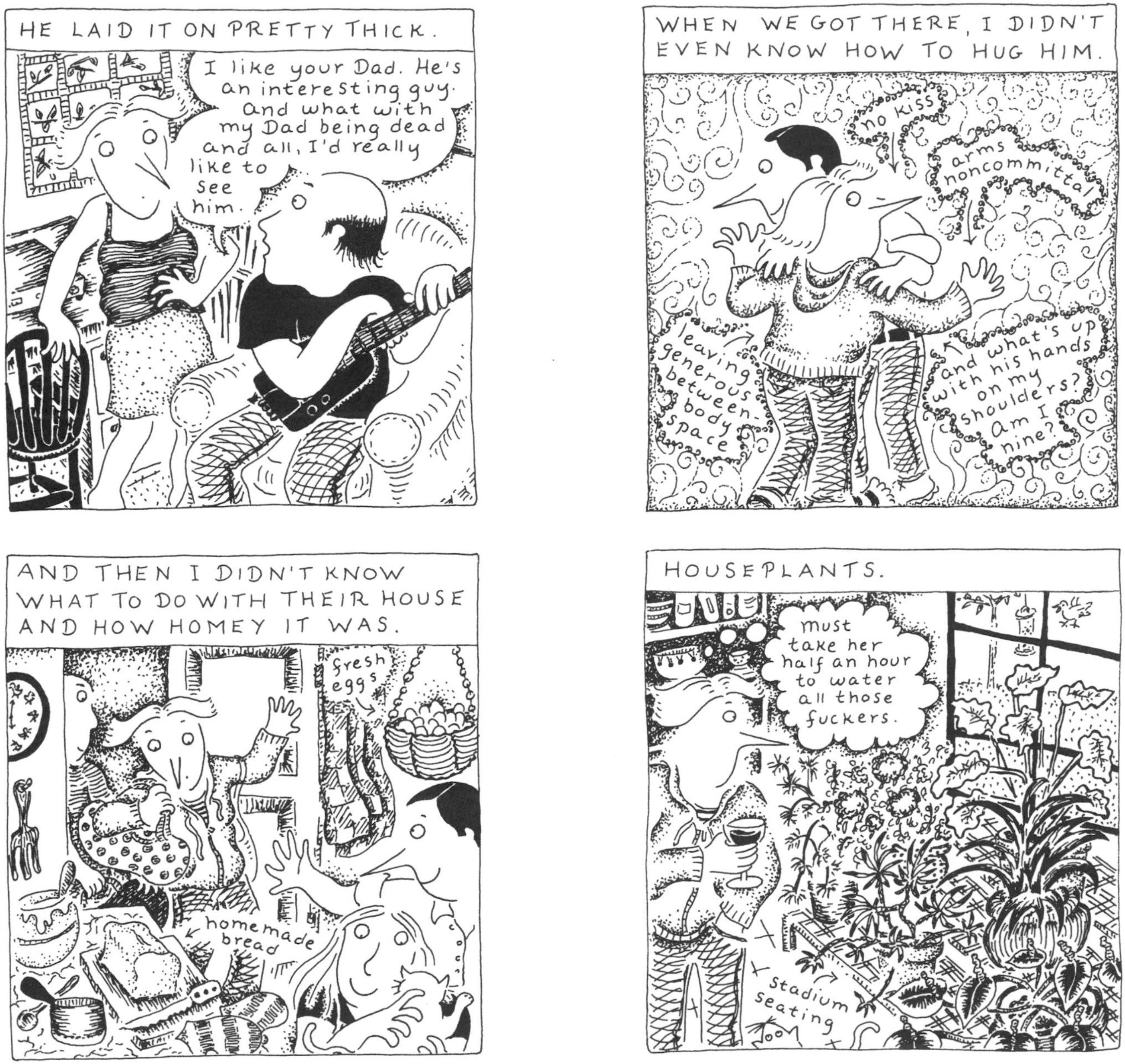
HE LAID IT ON PRETTY THICK.
I like your Dad. He's an interesting guy. And what with my Dad being dead and all, I'd really like to see him.
WHEN WE GOT THERE, I DIDN'T EVEN KNOW HOW TO HUG HIM.
no kiss
arms noncommittal
leaving generous between-body space
and what's up with his hands on my shoulders? Am I nine?
AND THEN I DIDN'T KNOW WHAT TO DO WITH THEIR HOUSE AND HOW HOMEY IT WAS.
fresh eggs
homemade bread
HOUSEPLANTS.
must take her half an hour to water all those fuckers.
stadium seating

CURTAINS.

AND THEY HAD A THING ABOUT CHICKENS.

THE THING THEY HAD FOR EACH OTHER HAD SURVIVED LEAVING EVERYTHING THEY'D LEFT BEHIND.

AND I ASKED MYSELF WHAT KIND OF A SHITTY DAUGHTER DOESN'T WANT HER DAD TO FIND THE SAME HAPPINESS SHE'S FOUND HERSELF.

Pretty serious fucking view, eh?

Really shitty, that's what.

SO, LIKE I SAID, THERE WE WERE, NOT TALKING MUCH, WALKING AROUND HIS NEW PLACE, WHEN WE REACHED A STREAM.

THERE WAS A FOOTBRIDGE OVER IT, MADE OF A COUPLE OF PLANKS.

rickety as shit

DAD OFFERED ME HIS ARM.

WHICH HE WOULDN'T ORDINARILY HAVE DONE, EXCEPT-

We don't want you falling.

I WAS SIX WEEKS PREGNANT BY THEN.

YUP.

MY TITS WERE SO SWOLLEN AND TENDER, I HAD TO HOLD ONTO THEM WHEN I DROVE OVER BUMPS IN MY CAR.

I SUPPOSE MY PREGNANCY WAS THE REAL REASON WE'D GONE UP THERE.

IT WAS A SMALL, CHIVALROUS GESTURE. BUT SOMEHOW IT SAID EVERYTHING I NEEDED TO KNOW.

HE'D NEVER STOPPED BEING MY FATHER.

Taking me to the schoolbus stop on his way to work

hat! really!

briefcase

Running to keep up

schoolbag

NO MATTER HOW HARD I'D TRIED TO STOP BEING HIS DAUGHTER.

I REACHED OUT, FLOODED WITH LOVE, AND TOOK HIS ARM.

AND WE GOT OVER THAT BRIDGE.

Thanks, Dad.

SEPTEMBER TOOK THE SUMMER, AND WITH IT ALICE'S MORE-THAN-THREE-YEAR GRACE PERIOD, SYMPTOM-FREE.

Mom, we heard you weren't doing too well.

No, as a matter of fact, I'm not.

SHE SAW ME BESIDE HIM IN THE DOOR.

Aren't you cute! Is that a new coat?

I couldn't button the old one anymore.

BACK LASH Susa Falud

STILL THIS UNFLAGGING ATTENTION TO THE LIVES AROUND HER.

Of course not. How far along are you?

Four months.

Look at you. You're starting to show.

JIM STEPPED IN.

Mom, are you going to tell us what's going on, or what?

Instantly, dear.

SHE SAID SHE'D BEEN TO A LECTURE AT THE UNIVERSITY THAT MORNING, AND WAS CLIMBING A FLIGHT OF STAIRS ON HER WAY OUT.

SUDDENLY SHE HAD TO SIT DOWN.

SHE COULDN'T CATCH A BREATH.

I was terrified.

FORD CAME AND TOOK HER TO THE HOSPITAL, WHERE THEY FOUND OUT HER LUNG HAD COLLAPSED.

AND THERE IT WAS: THE THING THAT CONTAINED THE END.

WHEN WE WOULDN'T BE ABLE TO TOUCH HER. BECAUSE SHE WOULD NO LONGER BE THERE.

Come. Perch. Tell me everything I've missed.

as always: chicken

AND AT LAST WE'D BE ON OUR OWN...

waving goodbye →

THE DOCTOR GAVE HER LESS THAN A YEAR.

I can't believe she's really going to die.

I can't believe I'm going to be a fucking orphan.

NOW, EVERYTHING WAS FOR THE LAST TIME.

AND FOR HER LAST CHRISTMAS, SHE DECIDED SHE WANTED TO GO TO VERMONT.

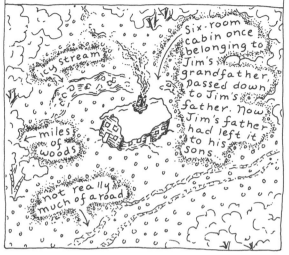

THE HOUSE WAS OFF THE GRID. IT HAD NEVER BEEN ON THE GRID. THERE WAS NO GRID UP THERE.

ALICE WAS REMEMBERING SUMMER VISITS, WHEN THEODORE'S DAD WAS STILL ALIVE AND THE BOYS WERE SMALL.

NOW, AT LEAST, JIM AND HIS BROTHERS HAD INSTALLED A GRAVITY FEED WATER SUPPLY AND A REAL TOILET.

I'd refused to go up there till they had a toilet

You sure this thing works?

BUT ALICE WAS CONCERNED ABOUT WHAT WE'D DO IF WE ALL GOT SNOWED IN UP THERE.

Fig. A - woman dying of lung cancer

What if I suddenly take a turn for the worse?

house

car car car

car

Fig. B - woman seven months pregnant (looks at least nine)

What if I go into labor?

SO FORD CAME UP WITH A PLAN.

IF ONE OF US NEEDED TO GET TO THE HOSPITAL, THEY'D LASH US TO THE OLD TOBOGGAN.

hypothetical

Hey! Wait a minute!

THEN THEY'D DRAG US DOWN THE SIDE OF THE MOUNTAIN.

AND THEY'D USE THE FARMER'S PHONE AT THE BOTTOM TO CALL AN AMBULANCE.

A RESCUE VEHICLE WOULD CART US OFF FROM THERE...

WITH THIS IN MIND, WE ALL DROVE UP A COUPLE OF DAYS BEFORE CHRISTMAS.

IT WAS TWENTY-FIVE BELOW.

THE SNOW WASN'T DEEP, BUT THE WINDOWS WERE HEAVILY FROSTED WITH ICE.

WE'D BEEN UP THERE IN JULY.

I HAD MORNING SICKNESS BY THEN, WHICH WAS LESS A PUKEFEST AND MORE AN ALL-DAY MARVELING AT HOW DISGUSTING I FELT.

213

NOW ALICE WAS THE ONE WHO FELT SICK, BECAUSE OF HER PAINKILLERS. SOMETIMES SHE'D SUDDENLY LOSE IT.

Did Ford tell you I barfed in a garbage can at the mall?

Oh, man. That really, really sucks.

WE TOOK OUR PILLS TOGETHER.

Prenatal vitamins

THE GUYS KEPT FEEDING THE FIRE IN THE WOOD STOVE THEY'D INSTALLED IN THE KITCHEN.

THERE WERE ROCKING CHAIRS ON EITHER SIDE.

214

WHICH ALICE AND I WERE GLAD TO FILL.

AND AS WE SAT AND ROCKED, I FELT THE LIFE THAT WAS SLOWLY LEAVING HER ALREADY-THINNING BODY ENTERING MINE.

WHERE IT SENT A FOOT LIKE A SHARK FIN SAILING ACROSS MY DOMED BELLY. MY SON.*

That's my boy!

* I'd had amniocentesis, because I'd be thirty-two when I delivered.

HE FELT MY SORROW THAT SHE MIGHT NEVER SEE HIM.

Hush, now.

quiet

WE CUT A TREE DOWN ON CHRISTMAS EVE.

WE LET THE SNOW MELT OFF IT IN THE BACK HALL FOR A COUPLE OF HOURS.

THEN WE DECORATED IT.

SOMEBODY LIT THE CANDLES.

216

SUDDENLY AN ENVELOPE TOO CLOSE TO A FLAME CAUGHT...

FIRE!

BUT WE DIDN'T, BECAUSE FISH UNFROZE NEXT TO HIS FLAMING CARD AND KNOCKED IT OFF THE TREE.

Holy shit!

AND WE STAMPED OUT EVERY LAST TRACE OF DEATH ON THE WOODEN FLOOR.

There's one!

There's another one over there!

CHAPTER TEN: Tits at Dawn

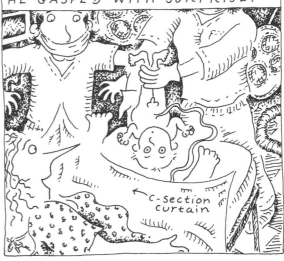

WHEN THEY PULLED HIM OUT THROUGH THE WALL OF MY UTERUS, HE GASPED WITH SURPRISE.

← c-section curtain

NO WONDER: FOR THE LAST TWENTY-FOUR HOURS I'D BEEN TRYING TO PUSH HIM OUT THE OTHER WAY.

His head isn't tucked in enough. His chin is getting stuck. I'll try to get him into position.

← my o.b. got up on the table with me.

Damn, woman.

BUT THEN I'D STARTED DOZING OFF BETWEEN CONTRACTIONS.

She's failing to progress. We're thinking about doing a c-section. How would you guys feel about that?

my ice chips

ZZZZ

JIM, WHO'D BEEN AT MY SIDE SINCE HE'D BROUGHT ME IN - WITH THE EXCEPTION OF A PANCAKE BREAK - WAS COOL WITH THIS.

DURING AN AWAKE MOMENT, I ALSO AGREED TO THE C-SECTION, EVEN THOUGH I FELT I WAS LETTING SOMEBODY DOWN.

BUT THEN I REALIZED I WAS BEING RIDICULOUS. HERE HE WAS. BEAUTIFUL. BREATHING. WET WITH FURLED-UP LIFE.

AND THEN I SLEPT. WHEN I WOKE UP, THEY'D PUT HIM IN MY ROOM.

219

IT WAS LIKE CHRISTMAS MORNING.
WHEN I WAS SMALL AND ALMOST
AFRAID OF ALL THAT JOY, THE
WAY IT TOWERED OVER ME.

FOR A LITTLE WHILE, I JUST
BREATHED ON THE EDGE OF
THE BED.

THEN I PICKED HIM UP AND
KISSED HIM AND NESTLED HIM
AGAINST MY SKIN.

WHEN HE WOKE UP AND
YAWNED, I TRIED TO NURSE HIM.

Oh, man, I don't think it's working.

IT WASN'T AS EASY AS IT LOOKED.

NOTHING WAS EASY.

BUT THERE WERE MOMENTS. LIKE WHEN JIM CAME TO VISIT ME ON THE WAY TO A GIG AND I GAVE HIM THE BABY TO HOLD.

AND LIKE THAT-IN THAT SECOND-JIM'S FACE CHANGED. SOFTENED. DEEPENED. HE BECAME A FATHER IN FRONT OF MY EYES.

FOUR DAYS AFTER MY C-SECTION, IT WAS TIME TO TAKE THE BABY HOME.

MOM WAS ALREADY IN THE DRIVEWAY.

How are you feeling, sweetie?

Oh my God, mom, I'm so glad to see you!

I MEANT IT. OF ALL THE PEOPLE IN THE WORLD, SHE WAS THE ONE I MOST WANTED TO SEE—THE ONE WHO'D GIVEN BIRTH TO ME.

WHILE MOM IN HER QUIET WAY DID THE LAUNDRY, THE GARBAGE, AND THE RECYCLING, I PUT THE BABY DOWN AND SLEPT.

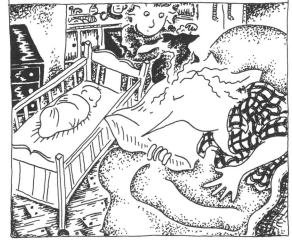

WE'D TOSSED OUR OLD SOFA AND GOTTEN A NICE LONG THREE-SEATER OUT OF STORAGE THAT HAD BELONGED TO MY GRANDMOTHER.

THE BABY SLEPT IN A LITTLE ROLLING CRIB MY MOM HAD USED FOR ALL OF US.

I JUST WASN'T READY TO DEAL WITH THE WHOLE SEPARATION THING YET.

WHEN THE BABY WOKE, JIM DIAPERED AND I NURSED.

THAT WAS OUR DIVISION OF LABOR BECAUSE THE BABY REFUSED TO TAKE A BOTTLE.

DINNER WAS SO GOOD, AND MOM POURED ME A GLASS OF WINE.

A FEW SIPS AND I WAS TRASHED.

BUT MOM WAS SO SYMPATHETIC.

WE DIDN'T HAVE ROOM FOR MOM, SO SHE HAD TO SLEEP IN THE OTHER HOUSE. FIVE MINUTES AFTER SHE LEFT, I BURST INTO TEARS.

SOB!!

JIM WAS HORRIFIED.

It's nothing. Just hormones. They told me I'd have a meltdown.

SOB!!

HE CIRCLED ME.

I mean - they give you this baby - and they let you take it home - and everyone thinks you can take care of it...

But what if I kill it?

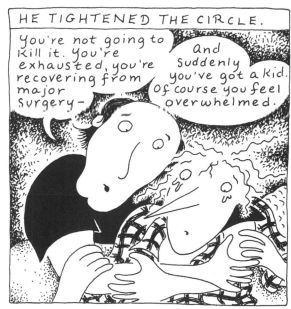

HE TIGHTENED THE CIRCLE.

You're not going to kill it. You're exhausted, you're recovering from major surgery-

And suddenly you've got a kid. Of course you feel overwhelmed.

225

THE STILL-SANE PART OF MYSELF TOLD THE CURRENTLY-CRAZY PART OF MYSELF TO BELIEVE HIM.

Besides, there are other people involved here. We're looking after it too. Nobody is going to let the baby die.

Ō Ō

Now give us a kiss and get some sleep.

HE TOOK THE BED AND I TOOK THE COUCH, AS AGREED, SINCE I HAD THE TITS AND HE NEEDED HIS SLEEP FOR GIGS AND TEACHING.

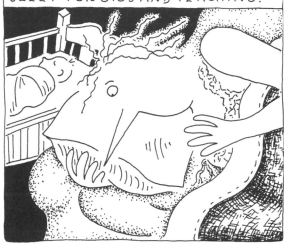

WE'D AGREED... BUT AS I LOOKED OUT THE DARK LIVING ROOM WINDOWS, MY CHEST FILLED WITH DREAD.

THE WINTER NIGHT. THE CHILL. THE AWFUL SILENCE. MY OWN MURDEROUS INCOMPETENCE.

I HAD TO WIN THIS WAR WITH MYSELF, IF IT TOOK ALL NIGHT. INSANELY, A LINE CREPT INTO MY HEAD FROM MACBETH.

THE WITCHES GAVE MACBETH THIS PROPHECY WHEN HE WAS WORRYING WHETHER HE'D KEEP HIS ILL-GOTTEN KINGDOM.

AND THEN IT HAPPENED.

THE SUN ROSE AND I REALIZED THE BABY AND I HAD DONE THE IMPOSSIBLE: WE'D MADE IT THROUGH THE LONG, DARK NIGHT.

THE COFFEE JIM MADE SMELLED LIKE THE SAFETY OF THE DAY.

Oh, thank God.

mom came over at breakfast time

How're you feeling?

AND IN THIS SAFETY, JIM AND I WALKED, WITH THE BABY, OVER TO THE OTHER HOUSE.

my do, all grown out now.

AND PLACED HIM IN ALICE'S ARMS.

JUST TWO WORDS, IN THE QUIET KITCHEN.

He's cute.

SHE WAS WEAKER NOW AND NEEDED OXYGEN. WHEN SHE'D VISITED US IN THE HOSPITAL, SHE WOULDN'T HOLD THE BABY.

You sure?

I COULD SEE HER REGRET.

I'm afraid I'll drop him.

It was a pretty long walk for her from the car.

BRIEFLY I COULD SEE THAT RARE THING, A FLICKER OF HER ONCE-BOTTOMLESS INTEREST IN OTHER PEOPLE.

Now, perch and tell me everything.

Wow.

I think you'd better take him.

TEN DAYS LATER, WE RELUCTANTLY GAVE MOM A RIDE TO THE BUS.

Darling, of course you'll survive without me.

Besides, your sister needs me back.

crossword puzzle

229

THERE WAS NO MORE PUTTING OFF BECOMING THIS PERSON I NEEDED TO BECOME.

OR PERHAPS IT HAD ALREADY HAPPENED.

I CARRIED THE BABY ACROSS THE LAWN TO SEE HER EVERY DAY.

HOPING, IMPOSSIBLY, TO PLANT THEIR MEMORIES OF EACH OTHER DEEP ENOUGH TO LAST.

THERE WAS NOW A BIG BOX IN THE DINING ROOM WITH A VERY LONG BREATHING TUBE, SO SHE COULD HAVE OXYGEN ALL THE TIME.

SHE BECAME FORGETFUL. THE CANCER HAD SPREAD TO HER BRAIN.

ONE DAY SHE ASKED ME TO BRING DOWN HER JEWELRY BOX.

LEMON TOPAZ DROP EARRINGS HER MOTHER HAD WORN ON HER WEDDING DAY.

AN AMETHYST NECKLACE CELEBRATING ALICE'S HIGH SCHOOL GRADUATION.

Headmaster of the school where her father taught

Thank you.

Her mom

Her Dad

AND HER PEARLS.

They may seem too heavy for you now. But later. Older. Feel right. Gutsy.

WHEN SHE COULDN'T TAKE THE STEPS ANYMORE, THEY MOVED HER BEDROOM DOWNSTAIRS.

SHE MADE THEM POSITION HER RENTED HOSPITAL BED SO IT FACED THE WINDOWS.

commode her mother had used when she broke her hip

SHE WASN'T SLEEPING MUCH.
SHE SAID SHE LIKED TO SEE
THE DAWN.

AND AFTER ALL SHE'D TAUGHT
US, IT SEEMED THAT NOW SHE
WAS GOING TO TEACH US HOW TO
DIE.

Here, Lambies.
I haven't
thought of
you in a
long
time.

MARY
1893-1895

THE HOSPICE PEOPLE CAME.
THEY GAVE HER AN
INTRAVENOUS MORPHINE DRIP.

You'll be more
comfortable. But
you'll sleep
more.

I DON'T THINK SHE WAS
SLEEPING. I THINK SHE WAS
TRAVELING.

Just don't expect
her to make sense.
Sometimes she
won't know
where she
is.

SHE MADE SENSE ONLY ONE MORE TIME WHEN JIM AND I WERE WITH HER.

JUST TWO WORDS, IN THE QUIET ROOM.

THE MORPHINE EASED HER INTO A COMA.

ONE NIGHT WE WERE ALL MAKING DINNER AT ALICE'S, AND I FOUND SANDY SITTING NEXT TO HER, READING ALOUD.

WHILE I READ, I LISTENED TO HER BREATHE.

AND I THOUGHT ABOUT ALL THE THINGS THAT HAD HAPPENED IN THAT ROOM.

ALL THAT LIVING.

AND NOW THIS DYING...

JIM'S FEET POUNDED UP THE STAIRS. HIS WILD FACE IN THE HALL. THE WORDS.

SHE'S DEAD!!

I SCOOPED UP THE BABY-I'D JUST PUT HIM DOWN FOR HIS NAP-AND WE RAN.

NOLI ME TANGERE.

ALL THE LIFE HAD AT LAST BEEN TAKEN FROM THE LIVELIEST WOMAN I HAD EVER KNOWN.

FOR THE FIRST TIME IN WEEKS WE LEFT ALICE ALONE AND WALKED TOGETHER OUTSIDE.

I HATED LEAVING HER THERE, AS WE BLINKED IN THE BRILLIANT SUNLIGHT.

TILL I REALIZED SHE WAS HERE. IN THE GRASS SHE'D MOWED, THE BRICKS SHE'D WEEDED, THE DIRT SHE'D DUG ON SUNDAYS.

WE WERE TOUCHING HER.

237

CHAPTER ELEVEN: momtits

FIVE JULYS.

GENEVA WAS TWO.

mirror they wheeled in so I could watch her birth

epidural

SMOOTHLY SHE SLID INTO THE WORLD, AND SMOOTHLY SHE MADE US A FAMILY.

No, you may **NOT** hit your sister when she's nursing.

light saber

JIM LEFT THE WEDDING BAND.

HE GOT A COUPLE OF JOBS TEACHING LESSONS AT LOCAL SCHOOLS.

I COULDN'T FIND ANY FREELANCE WRITING WORK AND DECIDED TO BECOME A HIPPIE INSTEAD.

I GREW MY HAIR LONG TO SAVE ON HAIRCUTS, PLANTED A VEGGIE GARDEN, AND SHOPPED AT YARD SALES.

239

HE THOUGHT I WAS DISAPPEARING, BUT I WAS ACTUALLY COMING INTO FOCUS.

JIM HELD MY SHOULDERS.

I'D GIVEN UP FREELANCE WRITING FOR ANOTHER REASON. AFTER GENEVA'S BIRTH, I'D BOUGHT MYSELF A PRESENT.

WRITING WAS GLAD TO SEE ME GO. DRAWING HAD REALLY, REALLY MISSED ME.

AND ONE AFTERNOON, I GOT IT. AS I WAS SITTING IN MY INKY JOY.

I've had both my kids...

Barring any unwanted pregnancies, the next big biological moment for me is death.

Before that happens, I'd be crazy not to try to make a living at this.

WE BURIED ICHABOD ON ANOTHER AFTERNOON.

JIM DUG A HOLE FOR HIM BY THE OLD SILO.

What happened to Icky to make him dead, though?

Old age, Teddy. Basically.

Fourth of July bike decoration

Vet death bag

GENEVA DID NOT EXACTLY ATTEND THE FUNERAL.

How's it going, Jenny?*

*We called her "Jenny" for short, even though the spelling was wrong.

241

SHE HAD SOME OTHER SHIT TO ATTEND TO.

THERE HAD BEEN A GLITCH IN HER POTTY TRAINING, SO NOW SHE WOULD ONLY CRAP OUTSIDE.

POOR JENNY, WHO ALWAYS GOT ME AT THE END OF A TIRED DAY.

JIM GAVE THE DOG ONE LAST PAT AND THEN LOWERED HIM INTO THE EARTH.

AND WE WEPT FOR HIM. AND WE WEPT FOR ALL OF THEM.

THEY WERE ALL AROUND US. AT LEAST THAT'S HOW IT FELT. THAT'S WHY WE HAD STAYED.

THE RENTER REMAINED IN THE TENANT HOUSE, FORD MOVED TO RHODE ISLAND, AND PAUL AND JIM BECAME THE NEW LANDLORDS.

PAUL HAD ONE STIPULATION FOR STAYING.

THANK. YOU.

Oh, Lordy, Paul. That is such a fucking relief. I do NOT want to live over there.

Why?

a) nightmare to clean b) shit breaking all the time due to old age c) ghosts

SO WE LIVED IN THE BARN AS ALWAYS, AND WHEN JENNY WAS BORN, MY MOTHER HELPED US BUILD AN ADDITION.

new wing in upstairs of adjoining garage

our first place

She helped with this

not with this

IT WAS IN TEDDY'S NEW BEDROOM THAT I HUGGED HIM GOODNIGHT ON MONDAYS, BEFORE I SPENT THE NEXT NIGHT IN THE CITY.

Oh, I'm going to miss you too, Sweetie. But it's just for one night.

I'll have my breakfast with Granny, and then I'll take the bus home.

Magic Schoolbus

DINOSAURS

I DIDN'T WANT TO GO EITHER. I WAS TAKING A NIGHT CLASS IN CHILDREN'S BOOK ILLUSTRATION AT AN ART COLLEGE ON THE WEST SIDE.

dorky hat

Walmart coat

Portfolio ordered online

hopelessly 90's bag

I WAS TERRIFIED.

ALTHOUGH I WAS PLEASED TO FIND OUT HOW MUCH STUPIDER COLLEGE STUDENTS HAD BECOME.

AFTER THE CLASS I'D CRASH IN THE SPARE ROOM OF MOM'S NEW, SMALL APARTMENT.

SHE AND DAD HAD FINALLY GOTTEN THE WORLD'S LONGEST DIVORCE.

245

DAD AND PAMELA WERE MARRIED.

EVERYONE WAS EITHER BEING BORN OR REBORN.

MY BODY, HOWEVER, WAS DEFINITELY NOT ON BOARD WITH ALL THIS RENEWAL.

I'D FINALLY HAD SOME PAINFUL VARICOSE VEINS REMOVED FROM MY LEG.

I'D ALSO HAD SURGERY ON A MILK DUCT WHICH HAD CLOGGED BY THE END OF BOTH BOUTS OF NURSING.

I just wish the doctor hadn't called it a "lumpectomy"...

you know it's going to be normal.

my friend Valerie

THAT DIDN'T KEEP ME FROM CALLING HIS HOME NUMBER AND BREAKING DOWN ON THE PHONE WITH HIS WIFE.

If he could just call me with the lab results... It's just that - Sniff - the lab closed before calling me and now - Sob - I can't find out till Monday.

Val's body was totally on board with the whole renewal thing - two kids and she looked fifteen.

HE CALLED. EVERYTHING WAS FINE. EXCEPT - CLEARLY - ME.

I must be going out of my mind.

Jim and I slept in separate rooms because of my snoring

I keep wondering when it'll be my turn for something awful to happen.

Why? Because you're mortal?

BECAUSE EVERYTHING WAS MORTAL.

Yeah, you care about a lot of people and they're depending on you.

You're halfway through your life and you want to know where it went.

Welcome to middle age!

Now would be an excellent time for you to stop being a chicken-shit.

247

CHAPTER TWELVE: TITS ON FILM

IT WAS DEAFENING.

I WOKE UP SCREAMING.

Oh my God oh my God oh my God

I WAS SURE THE WALL OF MY ROOM HAD EXPLODED AND FALLEN OFF THE SIDE OF THE HOUSE.

Oh my God oh my God

BUT WHEN I TURNED ON THE LIGHT, IT WAS JUST LIKE BEFORE.

I JUMPED OUT OF BED AND RAN.

EVERYBODY WAS FINE, BUT THERE WAS A SMELL.

A LOW BOLT HAD HIT THE FLASHING OUTSIDE JEN'S WINDOW, PASSED THROUGH HER WALL AND INTO THE OUTLET BY JIM'S BEDSIDE TABLE.

249

NOW I WAS TERRIFIED ALL OVER AGAIN.

WITH CLARITY I SAW WHAT THE LAST ELEVEN YEARS OF RAISING A FAMILY TOGETHER HAD BEGUN TO MAKE CLOUDY.

THE NEXT MORNING, JIM CALLED THE ELECTRICIAN, AS WELL AS OUR BUILDER, WHO CAME OUT A WEEK LATER TO FIX THE DRYWALL.

AFTER THE BUILDER WAS GONE, JIM TOLD ME WHAT HE'D SAID WHEN THEY WERE ALONE.

JIM SHOOK HIS HEAD.

I WAS SORRY THEY'D HAD TO GO THROUGH THAT. I WAS ALSO UNCOMFORTABLE.

MORE THAN UNCOMFORTABLE. CHILLY.

FOR SOME REASON, I TOLD THE KIDS I HAD A MAMMOGRAM THE NEXT DAY. TEDDY ASKED: WHAT'S A MAMMOGRAM?

AGAIN, THAT CHILL. THOUGH IT WAS GONE BY THE TIME I WENT TO MY APPOINTMENT, WHERE A WOMAN CRIED IN THE DRESSING ROOM.

Really. Everything's fine. The radiologist said you can go home.

THEY WERE TEARS OF PURE RELIEF.

I came yesterday, and they asked me to come back for another picture today. I was so scared!

BIT OF AN OVERREACTION, I WAS THINKING, WHEN THE NURSE CAME BACK AND SAID THEY WANTED A CLOSEUP OF MY RIGHT BREAST.

THE RADIOLOGIST WAS SMILING AT ME. I DIDN'T LIKE HIM. HE WAS TOO SHINY.

This is your lucky day!

THE WHOLE ROOM SEEMED
OVERLY SHINY TO ME.

HE SWITCHED ON THE LIGHT BOX.
I REALLY WANTED TO GET OUT
OF THERE.

MY INTESTINES WERE STARTING
TO SHAKE.

ALL THIS LIGHT, AND I COULDN'T
SEE A THING.

HE SMILED.

I'd like you to make an appointment with our breast specialist, Dr. Schultz. After she takes a look at these films, she'll be able to tell you more.

Oh.

JIM PUT HIS CHIN ON THE TOP OF MY HEAD.

Steady now. Hush. I'm sure lots of women get abnormal mammograms that turn out to be fine.

BUT I WAS ALREADY IN THAT DARK PLACE.

They can't all be fine.

Sshhh...

Someone has to be unlucky.

Why shouldn't it be me?

DR. SCHULTZ WAS COMFORTABLY MANLY. I BEGGED HER — IN MY HEAD — TO TELL ME THE RADIOLOGIST WAS CRAZY.

Ha! Ha! Ha! Pleomorphic WHAT?! The man must have been doing acid on his lunch break!

ha! ha! ha!

ha!

SLAP!

254

BUT SHE NEVER EVEN CRACKED A SMILE.

I agree with the radiologist. These calcifications do look suspicious.

And they cover a large area—about three quarters of your right breast.

THE ONLY PART OF MY BODY I COULD FEEL WAS MY BOWELS.

That's why I'd like to do a biopsy.

JIM HELD ME TIGHTER, ALWAYS TIGHTER, AND NEVER TIGHT ENOUGH.

I still have that

My luck is over. Somebody had biopsy.

Why shouldn't it be me?

HE SHOOK ME.

Will you stop saying that?

I can't. It's true.

255

I TOLD HIM ABOUT THE COLLEGE ALL-NIGHTER WHEN I RAN INTO A HALLMATE AT THE VENDING MACHINE IN THE LOBBY.

I just know I'm gonna fail this test.

EVERY UTTERANCE AT FOUR IN THE MORNING SEEMS EERILY SIGNIFICANT, ESPECIALLY IF YOU HAVEN'T SPOKEN TO ANYBODY FOR HOURS.

No. You're not. You're going to be fine.

Why do you say that?

BUT SHE WAS SO CALM. AND I'D LEARNED TO EXPECT THE TRUTH FROM PEOPLE FROM THE MIDWEST.

I don't know. You just seem like one of those people who will always be all right, no matter what happens.

I'D BEEN CARRYING THIS AROUND WITH ME FOR A LONG TIME.

I'm going to be okay. No matter what happens, I'm going to be okay...

BIG BAD WORLD

256

BUT NOW I WANTED TO CALL HER UP, WHEREVER SHE'D GONE AFTER GRADUATION, AND TELL HER SHE WAS WRONG.

I can't believe you took her seriously to begin with.

A WEEK LATER I WAS LYING FACE DOWN ON A HIGH TABLE.

MY RIGHT BREAST HUNG DOWN THROUGH A HOLE.

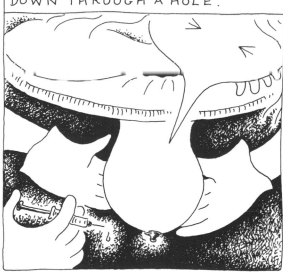

MY ARM WAS FOLDED UP LIKE A WING AS THEY GAVE ME A LOCAL.

Just a little pinch.

Yup.

IT STAYED THERE AS THEY STEERED THE BIOPSY NEEDLE, ATTACHED TO A COMPUTER, INTO MY BREAST, AGAIN AND AGAIN.

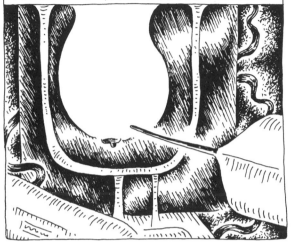

THE NEEDLE REMOVED SAMPLES OF THE SUSPICIOUS CALCIFICATIONS THEY COULD SEE ON MY MAMMOGRAM.

How are you feeling?

Actually, I'm in pain.

THERE WAS A GLOBAL NERVOUS PAUSE.

No, no, it's my arm. It's asleep.

Well, it **WAS** asleep. Now it's awake and it's killing me.

A LITTLE ARM MASSAGE AND SEVERAL SAMPLES LATER, THEY BANDAGED ME UP.

You can get dressed now.

THEY SAID GOODBYE WITH COMPASSION IN THEIR EYES. AND THE ONE THING I DIDN'T WANT TO HEAR –

Good luck!

OH, SHIT. I KNEW IT. I FAILED MY BIOPSY. THEY WERE TELLING ME I WAS DOOMED.

Jim's old Honda wagon, my third car. Sold my hatchback when baby seats were breaking my back in a two-door.

OF COURSE I WAS JUST BEING NUTS. HOW COULD THEY KNOW? NOBODY COULD.

We just have to wait for the results of my pathology.

God, it makes me sound so pathetic.

VALERIE GAVE ME THAT LOOK SHE HAD, AS THOUGH SHE WERE DIVING INTO MY SOUL AND BRINGING ME UP LIKE A PEARL.

You are NOT pathetic. You've been unbelievably strong about this.

Now, when are they going to call?

259

THANK GOD WE ALL HAD CELL PHONES BY THE SUMMER OF 2004.

This afternoon. Jim's teaching. I just couldn't face being with the kids at home alone.

SHE GAVE THE KIDS POPSICLES AND FED ME SANDWICHES AND TEA TILL MY PHONE STARTED RINGING IN MY PURSE.

You can use Dana's room. I'll keep them out.

Pops!

I am ass ring tone.

LAST TIME, I'D HAD TO STALK THE DOCTOR, THROUGH HIS WIFE. NOW I PRAYED IT WOULD BE THE NURSE, WITH GOOD NEWS.

Hello? This is Dr. Schultz.

OH, PLEASE, NO.

I have the results of your biopsy. All your samples contained DCIS, what we call Ductal Carcinoma In Situ.

Who ROCKS? DANA!

SHE WAS HARD TO HEAR BECAUSE OF THE POUNDING IN MY EARS.

What's Ductal Carcinoma In Situ?

SHE WAS ALSO HARD TO HEAR BECAUSE SHE WASN'T CALLING FROM HER OFFICE. SHE WAS ON HER CELL PHONE TOO.

It means a carcinoma that's still "in situ" or hasn't moved into the surrounding tissue.

IN THE BACKGROUND OF HER PHONE I COULD HEAR KIDS SCREAMING, LAUGHING. WAS THAT WATER SPLASHING?

It's essentially ██████████ If you're going to get breast cancer, this is the one to get.

I REALIZED SHE WAS CALLING FROM A SWIMMING POOL. FROM A LIFE I NO LONGER SHARED.

I just -I'm sorry- I have one more question. The thing I want to know is-

Can you tell me- if I have to lose the breast?

NOLI ME TANGERE

261

NOW HER VOICE WAS LOUD AND CLEAR.

Yes. The affected area is too large for us to salvage the breast. You will definitely have to have a mastectomy.

NOLi ME TANGERE

MY NIPPLES SHRIVELLED INTO BUDS OF TERROR AND I WAS SO COLD I WISHED I HAD A COAT.

I TOLD VAL. SHE HUGGED ME AND ASKED ME IF I WANTED TO GO HOME.

Yeah. I've got to tell Jim, and I don't want to do it over the phone.

IT WAS SO HARD TO DO THE MOST OBVIOUS THING. VAL STARTED COLLECTING OUR STUFF.

Listen, I just want you to know, whatever you have to do, you can drop the kids here any time of the day or night.

That's one thing you shouldn't have to think about.

262

SHE HUGGED ME ONE LAST TIME AND I DROVE MY KIDS AWAY FROM THAT PLACE OF HEALTH AND LIGHT.

INTO WHAT–?

It's going to be all right.

We're going to get through this.

All of us.

I LOVED HIS INFURIATING STUBBORNNESS SO MUCH RIGHT THEN.

I'm just so sorry, babe.

What the hell are you sorry for?

LEAVING YOU?

Putting you and the kids through this.

Especially after your mom... Both your parents.

Stop.

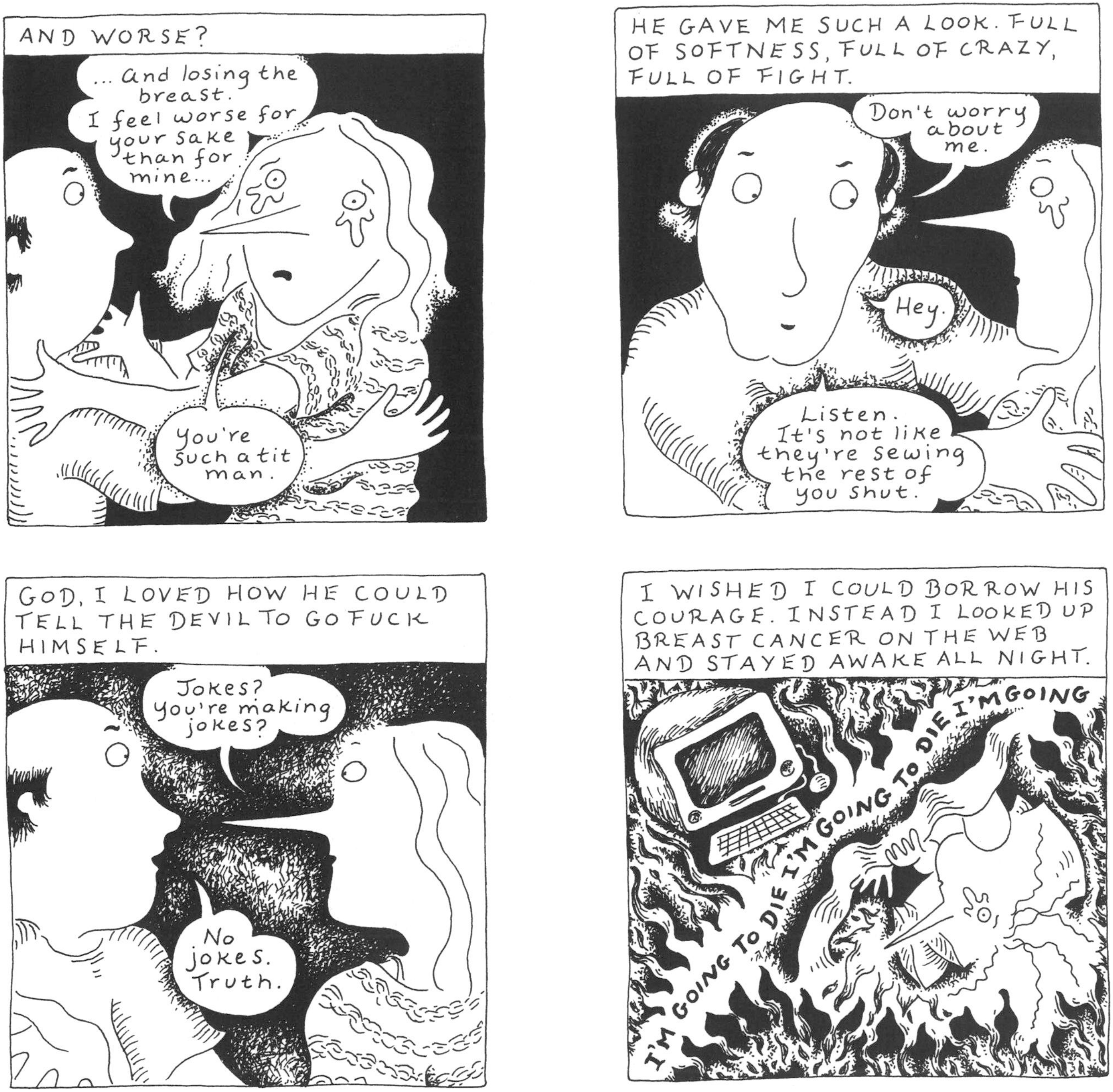
AND WORSE?
... and losing the breast. I feel worse for your sake than for mine...
You're such a tit man.
HE GAVE ME SUCH A LOOK. FULL OF SOFTNESS, FULL OF CRAZY, FULL OF FIGHT.
Don't worry about me.
Hey.
Listen. It's not like they're sewing the rest of you shut.
GOD, I LOVED HOW HE COULD TELL THE DEVIL TO GO FUCK HIMSELF.
Jokes? You're making jokes?
No jokes. Truth.
I WISHED I COULD BORROW HIS COURAGE. INSTEAD I LOOKED UP BREAST CANCER ON THE WEB AND STAYED AWAKE ALL NIGHT.
I'M GOING TO DIE I'M GOING TO DIE I'M GOING TO DIE I'M GOING

REMEMBERING THE LIGHT UNDER ALICE'S DOOR.

Is this why you taught us how to die? Because you knew it would be my turn soon?

BOOK OF THE DEAD

I WAS CONSTANTLY ASKING HER ADVICE IN MY DREAMS, BUT ALL SHE EVER DID WAS SMILE.

BOOK OF THE DEAD

BOOK OF THE DEAD

IN THE MORNING IT WAS TIME TO TELL MY MOTHER.

It's breast cancer. DCIS. Do you think that might be what you had?

At 78, finally starting to look her age

I'm sorry, dear. I just don't remember.

AND THEN I SAID THE THING I KNEW WOULD EMBARRASS HER, BUT I NEEDED HER TO HEAR ME SAY IT.

Mom. I just want you to know—it's not your fault.

HER VOICE SNAPPED WITH PAIN AND LOVE:

AND THEN, THE THING I NEEDED TO HEAR MYSELF SAY MORE THAN I NEEDED HER TO HEAR ME SAY IT.

BLESS HER.

I ALSO TOLD THE SMALL PUBLISHER THAT HAD HIRED ME TO ILLUSTRATE MY FIRST CHILDREN'S BOOK.

WITH SOME OF THE ADVANCE, I HAD RENTED A STUDIO SO THE KIDS COULDN'T BOTHER ME WHILE I WAS WORKING.

THE PUBLISHER WAS COOL ABOUT IT. SHE TOLD ME TO TAKE AS MUCH TIME AS I NEEDED.

I COULDN'T IMAGINE GETTING BACK TO WORK. I WAS SORRY I'D EVER RENTED THE STUDIO.

IT HAD TAKEN ME AWAY FROM MY CHILDREN.

267

THEY WERE THE ONES I COULD NOT TELL.

NOT TILL I KNEW EXACTLY WHAT I HAD TO TELL THEM.

I WON'T BE ABLE TO TAKE CARE OF YOU, TO GIVE YOU MY LOVE... I WON'T BE ABLE TO WATCH YOU GROW UP AFTER ALL?

OR: I HAVE TO GO THROUGH SOMETHING, BUT AFTERWARDS I WILL WRAP MYSELF AROUND YOU FOR THE REST OF OUR LIVES.

I'D ALWAYS BEEN SO OPEN WITH THEM. NOW I WAS HIDING FROM THEM THE GREATEST FEAR AND GRIEF I'D EVER KNOWN.

AND IT FELT AS IF I WERE WATCHING THEM THROUGH GLASS.

IT WAS SUCH A RELIEF - AND I FELT GUILTY ABOUT THAT - WHENEVER WE DROPPED THEM OFF AT CAMP VALERIE.

JIM AND I WOULD FINALLY GET A CHANCE TO TALK ON THE WAY TO MY APPOINTMENT.

HE'D SUGGESTED I FIND A SURGEON AT A BIGGER CANCER PLACE - IN EITHER NEW YORK OR PHILLY.

But - I know this is stupid - how will I get there? At least I can drive to Dr. Schultz's office.

USUALLY IRRITATED BY HOW I'D NEVER GOTTEN OVER MY HIGHWAY DRIVING PHOBIA, JIM CUT ME OFF WITH A LOOK OF SOFT, WARM CALM.

I'll take you wherever you want to go.

Whenever you need to go there.

I LEANED MY HEAD AGAINST HIS ARMOR.

I'm so glad you're the one I'm going to go through this with.

I HADN'T WANTED TO GO TO THAT BEHEMOTH SLOAN-KETTERING, SO HERE WE WERE, ON OUR WAY TO A PLACE OUTSIDE PHILLY.

I'm just so tired.

Still not sleeping?

THEODORE'S GIRLFRIEND CLAUDIA HAD GONE THERE FOR HER BREAST CANCER TREATMENT AND HAD RECEIVED EXCELLENT CARE.

It's just so tiring to have all these interruptions. I can't concentrate on anything anymore.

You don't have to. I can.

SOUTH
95

WE WERE GOING TO SEE A BREAST SURGEON FOR A SECOND OPINION, AND TO SEE IF I LIKED HER BETTER THAN DR. SCHULTZ.

We were really lucky she'd see us on such short notice. Paul pulled some serious strings for us.

Who's Paul, again?

BEEP!

Drummer. Works in health administration. He used to work here - and he says she's the best.

PARKING AREA F

WE GAVE THEM MY PATHOLOGY REPORT AND FILMS. I SAW A YOUNG GUY IN A WHEELCHAIR WITH A BALD HEAD, A BUCKET ON HIS LAP.

God, he looks so miserable... Brain tumor, you suppose...?

He's probably doing chemo...

THE BREAST SURGEON AGREED WITH DR. SCHULTZ ONE HUNDRED PERCENT.

Full mastectomy of the right breast. Also, a sentinel node biopsy.

Oh my God, what's THAT?

271

SHE WAS IMPRESSIVE. CONFIDENT. BUT COLD.

The removal of the first few lymph nodes near the breast...

...The so-called sentinel nodes, that would contain the cancer if it had spread.

SPREAD?

I thought DCIS meant it was still contained!

Sorry I can't help it pa—

There could be other types of cancer as well. We won't know that till after we section the breast tissue.

ON OUR WAY OUT, I SAW THE WOMAN WHO'D BEEN HELPING THE BALD GUY IN THE WHEELCHAIR. SHE WAS SMOKING A CIGARETTE.

AREA C

I JUMPED INTO THE CAR AND SLAMMED THE DOOR.

I'm sorry. I know your friend pulled strings and everything...

But I can't go here.

I'st just too depressing.

INSTEAD I CHOSE A PLACE THAT HAD A LOGO WITH A LITTLE GREEN LEAF.

THE LEAF GAVE ME HOPE THAT BREAST CANCER WOULD BE PART OF MY LIFE AND NOT THE END OF IT.

THE PLACE WAS ATTACHED TO THE TEACHING HOSPITAL IN PHILLY WHERE ALICE HAD GONE FOR HER LUNG CANCER TREATMENT.

THIS TIME FORD HAD PULLED STRINGS FOR US. HE'D CALLED ALICE'S ONCOLOGIST, WHO'D MOVED FROM A LUNG TO A BREAST SPECIALTY.

HE'D AGREED TO SEE US RIGHT AWAY.

I've reviewed your material. What I'd like to do is examine you. Then we can discuss your options.

AND THAT WAS THE FIRST TIME I SHOWED MY TITS TO A ROOM FULL OF STRANGERS.

I hope you don't mind. This is a teaching hospital, and these students are here to observe the exam.

all guys

SOMEHOW, I THOUGHT I WOULD ENJOY IT MORE.

TAKE IT OFF!!!

WOO!!

drooling

yawn

smack!

gag!

MAYBE THE PROBLEM WAS: I KNEW IT WAS FOR THE LAST TIME.

Thank you— you can get dressed now.

OR MAYBE IT WAS THAT MY TITS HAD CHANGED OVERNIGHT FROM SEXY FLESH MOUNTAINS TO POISONOUS DEPOSITS OF FAT.

NOW I EVEN SAW OTHER WOMEN'S TITS LIKE THAT.

WHICH WAS WHY I TOLD DR. WOLF I'D LIKE TO HAVE A BILATERAL MASTECTOMY - BOTH SIDES, NOT JUST THE ONE.

HE NODDED.

THEN HE LOOKED VERY SERIOUSLY INTO MY FACE.

But I want you to be certain of this decision. So I'm going to ask you to give me your reasons.

I LOOKED RIGHT BACK AT HIM.

Okay. First of all, my mother had breast cancer. So it's in my family.

Second, I'm relatively young. I'll recover better from the surgery now than if I have to have it done again at sixty-five.

Third, I'd rather have surgery than the long-term effects of radiation and chemo.

HE NODDED AGAIN.

And fourth is a stupid reason, but my mom's breasts after her mastectomy were never the same size.

Her prosthesis was always too small.

I'd like to reconstruct both my breasts at the same time so they match.

ONE BIG NOD.

You've thought it through. Good.

Let's schedule you for a bilateral mastectomy with a sentinel node biopsy—and reconstruction.

276

A QUIET DINNER AT OUR FAVORITE RESTAURANT, THE OARSMAN, BEFORE WE PICKED UP THE KIDS AT VAL'S.

I'D TOLD EVERYBODY BY NOW. MY BROTHER, WHO TOLD MY SISTER. MY FATHER, WHOSE WIFE HAD CREPT INTO MY HEART.

short hair now

We're just so **SORRY** you have to go through this. **PLEASE.** If there's anything at all we can do!

Just can't bring himself to say this shit

I'D EVEN TOLD THE MOTHER OF JEN'S BEST FRIEND KATHY. BUT NOT THE KIDS. NOT JEN AND TEDDY. NOT TILL I WAS CORNERED.

Mom, why did Kathy's mom ask me where I was staying while you were going to be in the hospital?

WE WERE ALL WATCHING A MOVIE IN THE LIVING ROOM.

Are you going to the hospital?

Oh, honey, yes, I am. I was waiting till I was sure. But now I need to tell you guys about it.

277

AND SUDDENLY, I HAD TO PERFORM.

Put it on **HOLD**, Dammit. Mom's talking to both of you, you know.

You remember that day I told you I was getting a mammogram? Well, it showed I have the same thing Grandma had. So I need to have the same operation.

I'M DAMAGING THEM, I'M DAMAGING THEM, OH PLEASE DON'T LET ME BE DAMAGING THEM.

I have to have my boob removed on this side. The same side as Grandma's! And I decided, to be sure I never get it again, to ask them to do the other boob as well.

Then they'll put in fake boobs, so I'll look a little better.

THAT WAS IT. JEN NODDED AND KEPT HER THUMB IN HER MOUTH; TEDDY ASKED IF WE COULD WATCH AGAIN; JIM SQUEEZED MY HAND.

Nicely done, Mom... I mean it.

IT WAS ABOUT ALL I COULD DO. WHILE HE SPENT HIS TIME ON THE PHONE, TRYING TO GET ME THE EARLIEST SURGERY DATE POSSIBLE.

Okay, I spoke to Dr. Wolf's office. He's looking for a surgeon who can operate in August, so you'll be all right by the time the kids are in school. And I made an appointment for your pre-op physical.

He's got his clipboard

Jim, I really don't know what I would do if you weren't here.

HE LEFT ME FREE TO DEAL WITH MY EMOTIONS. TO CALL THE NAMES ON A LIST I'D BEEN GIVEN. TO HAVE LUNCH IN A STRANGER'S KITCHEN.

I WAS AMAZED BY THE WAY SHE OPENED UP, JUST FOR THE SAKE OF HELPING ME THROUGH THIS.

SHE WIPED HER EYES AND WE TALKED A LITTLE ABOUT THE PROCEDURE.

THEN SHE ASKED IF I'D LIKE TO SEE HER BREASTS. I WASN'T SURE, BUT SUDDENLY HER SHIRT WAS IN THE AIR.

279

I WAS HORRIFIED. SOMEHOW THAT WAS WHEN I TRULY UNDERSTOOD THAT THIS WOULD BE MY CHEST.

But how will I be the same person?

I'D CALLED ANOTHER NUMBER I'D BEEN GIVEN, BELONGING TO A THERAPIST WHO'D HAD A MASTECTOMY HERSELF.

You won't be the same person.

But you will go on.

AND I TOLD HER HOW I'D SEEN A PAMPHLET IN A DOCTOR'S OFFICE THAT SAID, "CANCER IS NOT A PUNISHMENT."

Which is so stupid, but I do feel as though I need to find something to blame.

Chest x-rays for scoliosis? The milk duct they took out? Genetics?

Or was it something in my environment?

SHE ASSURED ME I'D NEVER KNOW AND THAT IT WAS FRUITLESS TO WONDER.

But if I don't know what caused it, how do I know what changes to make?

A PAUSE, LIKE A CONDUCTOR WITH HER BATON IN THE AIR.

You will make the changes that resonate.

That resonate.

CODA.

And, there's something a friend told me before my surgery.

You can say no - to an invitation or a request -

Without **ANY** explanation. Just say no. The answer's simply no.

No.

No. No. No.

SHE GAVE ME A MEDITATION CD. IT ASKED ME TO VISUALIZE MY HEALTHY CELLS CARRYING THE CANCER CELLS OUT OF MY BODY.

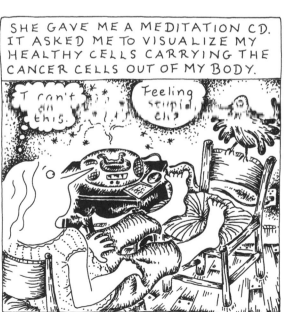

I can't do this.

Feeling stupid, eh?

THEN THE CD ASKED ME TO ENLIST THE HELP OF A HIGHER POWER. ANYTHING BIGGER OR STRONGER THAN I WAS.

But I don't believe in God. How can I -

AND THERE SHE WAS.

I'D BOUGHT HER RECENTLY AT THE BEAD STORE BECAUSE I'D RECOGNIZED HER FROM MY OLD ART HISTORY BOOK.

I thought so.

metal pendant with a loop on the back of her neck

Neolithic Europe: Fertility Goddess from Cernavoda, Romania. c. 5,000 B.C.E. Baked clay, 6 1/4" high.

NOW FLESH AND BLOOD, SHE COMFORTED ME. HEADLESS, MOUTHLESS, STILL, SHE WAS SPEAKING.

Put your head on my shoulder. Hear me. You are going to have to give up your breasts. Yes, you will suffer. But afterwards— I cannot tell you how— everything will be all right...

A CHUCKLE, A WHISPER, AS SHE FELL AWAY...

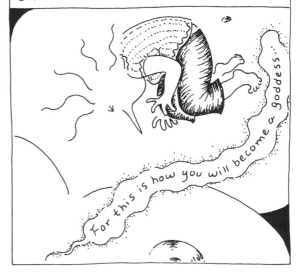

For this is how you will become a Goddess...

I DECIDED IT DIDN'T MATTER. THE IDEA WAS HEALING, EITHER WAY. SO I HELD ON TIGHT AND GAVE HER MY BELIEF.

I ALSO PROMISED I'D STRING HER PENDANT AROUND MY NECK.

IN GRATITUDE. FOR BEING THERE WHEN I NEEDED EXTRA STRENGTH.

TWO DAYS BEFORE MY OPERATION WE DROVE THE KIDS INTO THE CITY SO MY BROTHER COULD GIVE THEM A RIDE TO THE CAPE.

Thanks so much, babe.

Don't worry, we'll look after them.

JIM HAD INSISTED. HE WANTED ME TO RECOVER IN PEACE. MY MOM AND MY SISTER AGREED TO TAKE THEM FOR A COUPLE OF WEEKS.

THAT MORNING, JEN HAD KISSED MY BREASTS GOODBYE.

Thank you for giving me milk. We'll miss you!

NOW I KISSED MY CHILDREN GOODBYE.

Sweetie, take care of your sister.

You may be a big boy, but she's pretty upset.

ON THE LAST DAY I HAD TITS ON THIS EARTH, I PAINTED THEM YELLOW, WITH ORANGE NIPPLES.

I PAINTED THEM ORANGE, WITH GREEN NIPPLES.

I PAINTED THEM RED, WITH YELLOW NIPPLES.

THEN I RINSED OFF, MY TEARS BECOMING THE WATER I SWAM IN, RED PAINT RIBBONING AWAY FROM ME LIKE BLOOD.

285

FOUR A.M.
No Food! No WATER! CHECK-IN 7:00!!
THE STREETS WERE ASLEEP, BUT THE WAITING ROOM WAS WIDE AWAKE.
What are you here for?
Mastectomy.
SHE NODDED.
Same here. already had one. Came back in the other breast.
I WAS BECOMING AWARE OF LITTLE ELSE OTHER THAN MY HUNGER AND THIRST... THE DOCTORS WERE ARGUING.
But there is the dye. I can see it. She has a sentinel node at the top of her breast.
It's impossible! The lymph nodes must be located in the armpit.
not water
Why can't they shut the fuck up?
not food

THEY DID SOMETHING TO MY RIGHT BREAST - THE PAIN WAS A NICE BREAK - AND THEN CAREFULLY ADMINISTERED A BANDAID.

They're lopping this tit off in like an hour, but they put this nice little bandaid on it to, what, keep it from getting infected?

a little punchy, then, are we?

THERE WAS A GUY ON AN ELEVATOR WITH A BIG MAC.

his lunch

hospital ensemble

patient ensemble

MY SURGEON WAS A TINY SWEET LITTLE ADORABLE CHINESE LADY.

yes, it's nice to meet you too. We're going to give you some fluids to make you comfortable and a little something to help you relax.

I really, **REALLY** love your hair.

medi-Barcalounger

MY BRAIN SEEMED TO HAVE CRASHED INTO THE BOTTOM OF A VERY STEEP CLIFF.

Dude, I'm so fucking out of they'd just put me under.

Hang in there, party girl. The hard stuff's on the way.

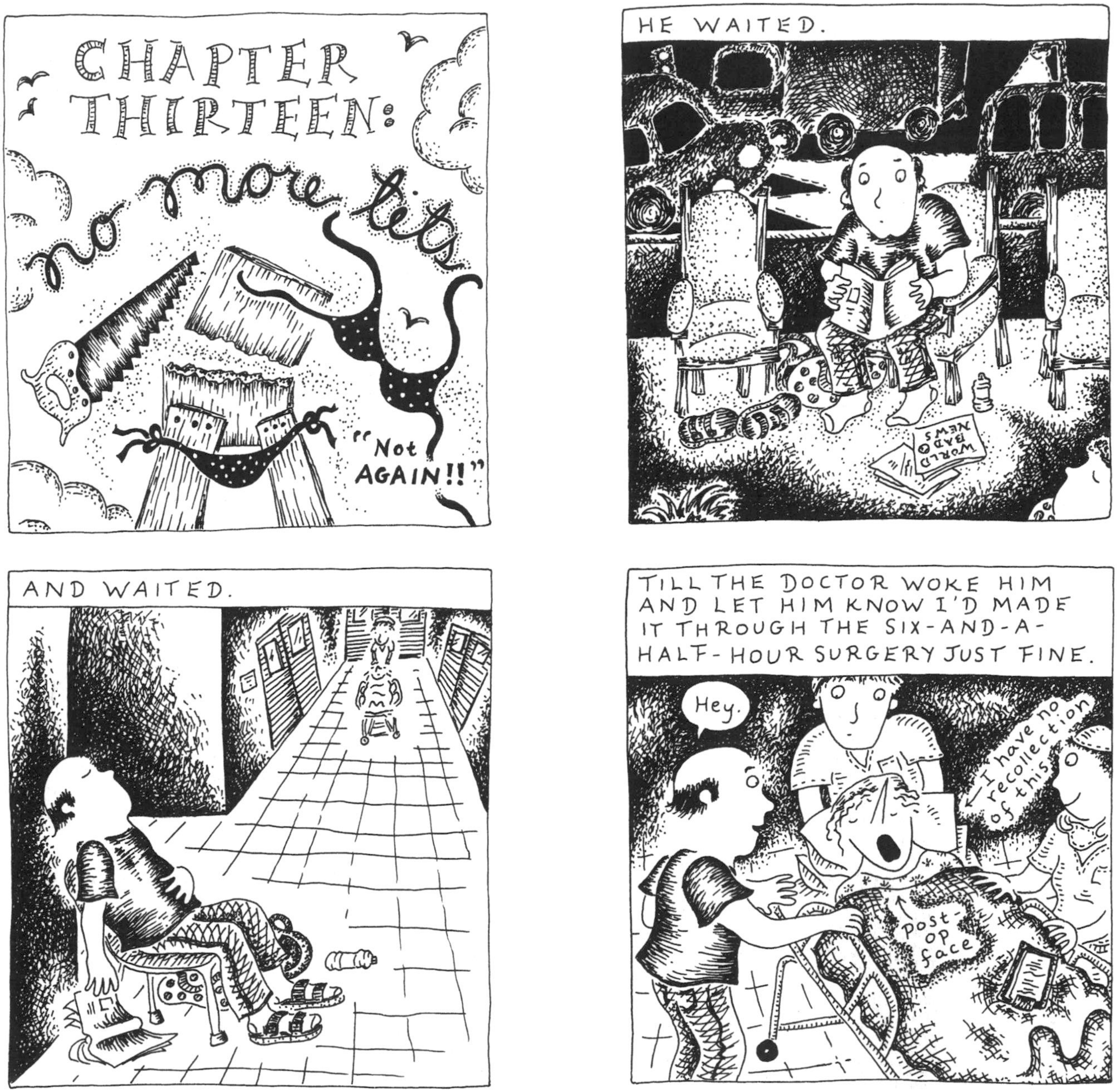
CHAPTER THIRTEEN:
no more tits
"Not AGAIN!!"
HE WAITED.
WORLD BAD NEWS
AND WAITED.
TILL THE DOCTOR WOKE HIM AND LET HIM KNOW I'D MADE IT THROUGH THE SIX-AND-A-HALF-HOUR SURGERY JUST FINE.
Hey.
I have no recollection of this.
post-op face

THE FIRST THING I REMEMBER IS FIGHTING MY WAY UP THROUGH THE MORPHINE.

THERE WAS TOO MUCH OF IT.

Press this button...

You have to keep pressing it...

A FACE BENDING OVER ME, A HAND TOUCHING ME, AND ON HER BOSOM A NECKLACE WITH A PINK RIBBON.

Did you have—?

Yes.

GRATITUDE.

MY SURGEON WAS THERE. SHE WAS ANGRY. SHE WAS SCOLDING SOMEONE ELSE IN THE ROOM.

A GUY MUMBLING SOMETHING IN THE BACKGROUND.

I WOKE. I HAD TO GET UP TO PEE. MY CHEST DIDN'T HURT, BUT USING THE MUSCLES IN MY ARMPITS WAS AGONIZINGLY PAINFUL.

FOR A LITTLE WHILE, I JUST BREATHED ON THE EDGE OF THE BED.

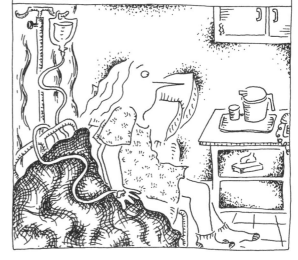

THEN I LOOKED DOWN AT THE FLAT BANDAGE AROUND MY CHEST.

covered by a 32 AA front clasp white cotton bra ←

AND I WAS SO RELIEVED.

THE TOXIC PUDDLES OF FAT ON MY CHEST WERE GONE, AND THEY COULDN'T SPREAD THEIR POISON TO MY BODY ANYMORE.

NO FLESH UP FRONT FLOPPING AROUND, GETTING IN MY WAY, TRYING TO CATCH UP WITH THE REST OF MY BODY'S MOVEMENTS.

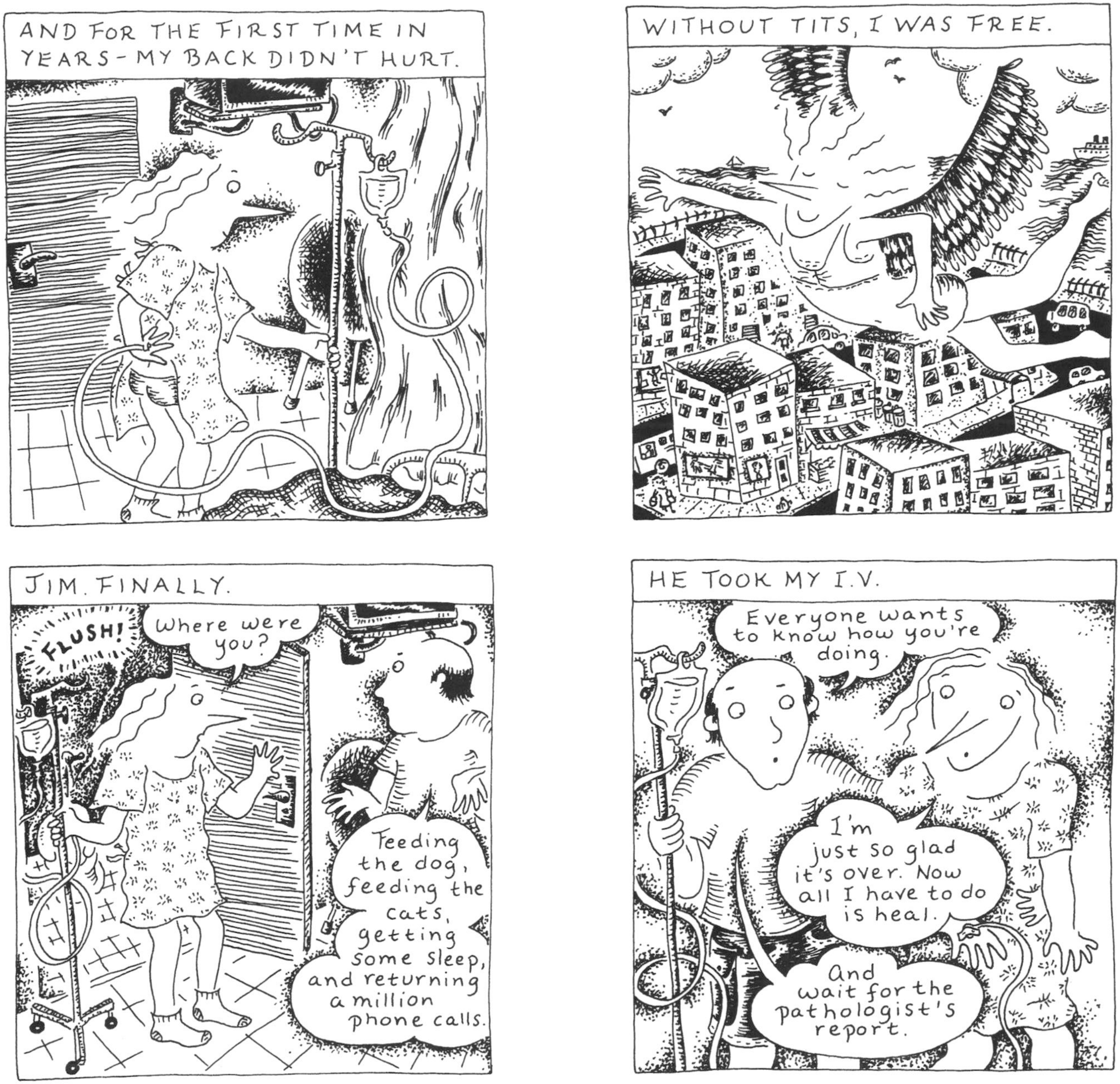
AND FOR THE FIRST TIME IN YEARS - MY BACK DIDN'T HURT.
WITHOUT TITS, I WAS FREE.
JIM. FINALLY.
FLUSH!
Where were you?
Feeding the dog, feeding the cats, getting some sleep, and returning a million phone calls.
HE TOOK MY I.V.
Everyone wants to know how you're doing.
I'm just so glad it's over. Now all I have to do is heal.
And wait for the pathologist's report.

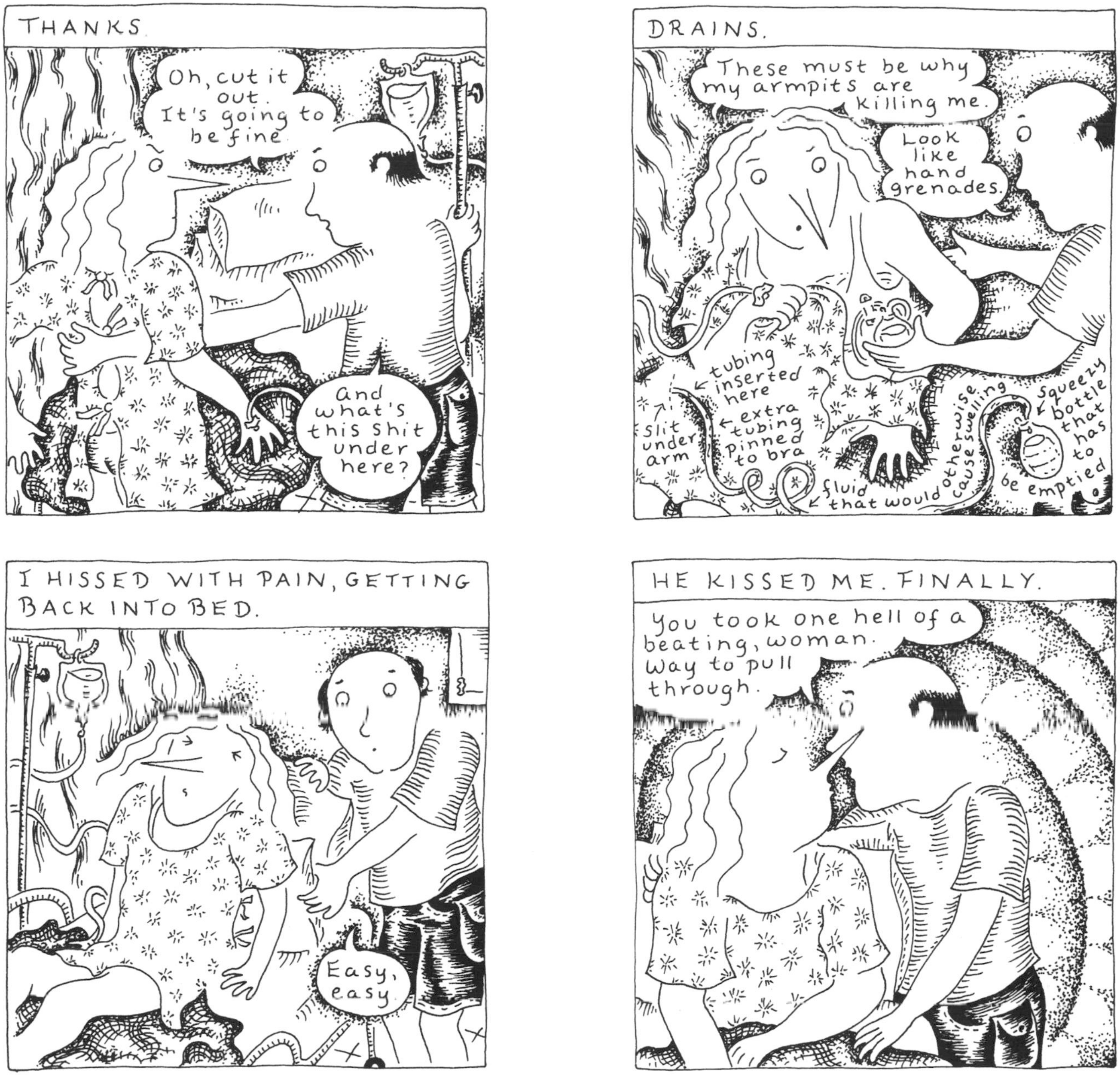
THANKS.
Oh, cut it out. It's going to be fine.
And what's this shit under here?
DRAINS.
These must be why my armpits are killing me.
Look like hand grenades.
tubing inserted here
slit under arm
extra tubing pinned to bra
fluid that would otherwise cause swelling
squeezy bottle that has to be emptied
I HISSED WITH PAIN, GETTING BACK INTO BED.
Easy, easy.
HE KISSED ME. FINALLY.
You took one hell of a beating, woman. Way to pull through.

NIGHT. FEAR. THEN ANGER. I WOKE TO FIND MY HAND SWOLLEN UP LIKE A SURGICAL GLOVE FILLED WITH WATER.

JESUS!

Where the FUCK are all the nurses?

I lost my tits, but I am NOT going to lose my HAND!!

PUSH! PUSH! PUSH! PUSH! PUSH! PUSH! PUSH!

NO ONE CAME, SO I WANDERED DOWN THE HALL, WHERE I PASSED DOOR AFTER SCARY DOOR WITH WARNING SIGNS ABOUT DISEASES.

NO EXIT

man, these people are sick.

BIO HAZARD

STOP! GOWNS & GLOVES REQUIRED

CAUTION RADIATION AREA

BACK OFF! WILDLY INFECTIOUS

THE ONE CHICK LEFT AT THE NURSE'S STATION BARELY EYEBALLED MY GLOVE-HAND.

We're having a busy night.

Yeah, this happens when the i.v. gets knocked out of position.

DE-FIBRILL-ATOR

I'll send someone to reset it for you.

SO I SKULKED BACK TO MY ROOM. MY ROOMMATE WAS AWAKE. WE STILL HADN'T OFFICIALLY SAID ANYTHING TO EACH OTHER YET.

You're here for a mastectomy. I heard you talking to your husband.

Yeah. What are you in for?

294

SHE WAS SO YOUNG. TWENTIES. TEENS? YET HER FACE WAS AS WASHED OF EXPRESSION AS A SMOOTH, PLUMP RIVERSTONE.

I FELT THE GODDESS PRETTY CLOSE BY RIGHT THEN. WITHIN EARSHOT OF MY THOUGHTS. SO I OFFERED THEM TO HER.

IT WAS THERAPEUTIC FOR ME TO THINK THIS WAY. THE FIRST BOOK I READ WHILE RECUPERATING WAS "I AM THE CENTRAL PARK JOGGER."

I THOUGHT IF MEILI COULD COME BACK FROM THAT, THEN I'D SNAP BACK FROM THIS SHIT IN NO TIME.

THE SECOND BOOK I READ WAS SOMETHING CALLED A GRAPHIC NOVEL. I'D SEEN AN ARTICLE AND HAD BOUGHT A FEW.

I FELT THIS DEEP STIRRING. CLARITY. CERTAINTY. THE ALMOST SEXUAL HEAT OF IGNITION.

I'D ALREADY DECIDED TO WRITE THIS STORY DOWN, BUT DOUBTED MY ABILITY WITH WORDS. NOW, IF I COULD DRAW PICTURES TOO—

CURRENTLY, HOWEVER, EVERYTHING WAS NOT ALL RIGHT. JEN WAS CALLING EVERY NIGHT IN TEARS.

I THOUGHT A LETTER MIGHT HEAD OFF THE TEARS, ESPECIALLY IF IT WAS FUNNY. SO I WROTE ONE. WITH PICTURES.

WHAT HE REALLY SAID WAS:

I'D PROBABLY NEVER LOOKED SO PITIFUL IN OUR LIFE TOGETHER. JIM TILTED HIS HEAD AT ME, THEN YANKED OPEN HIS CLOSET DOOR.

AND - PRESTO - I WAY WAS MORE PITIFUL.

Surgitape still covering my stitches

medical waste gunbelt

Okay, let's hit the showers!

IT IS NORMAL IN A LONG RELATIONSHIP TO DOUBT THE LOVE WE HAVE FOR EACH OTHER, THE NEED WE HAVE FOR EACH OTHER —

THEN ONE SMALL MOMENT OF NEED, OF TENDERNESS, AND EVERYTHING BUT THE LOVE IS WASHED AWAY.

AND HERE YOU ARE AGAIN, AND YET YOU'RE IN A BRAND NEW PLACE.

Kiss me, you fool. You know, that was the most romantic thing you've ever done for me.

Oh come on.

Wasn't there some shit back there about in sickness and in health?

298

HE HUNG THE TIE UP TO DRY.

For next time.

AND I PUT ON THE NEW KIMONO BATHROBE I'D ORDERED ONLINE.

Japanese, floor length, cotton, with real pocket sleeves

I GOT THE ONE WITH DRAGONS ON IT TO GIVE ME STRENGTH, LUCK, AND FORTUNE, AND TO WARD OFF EVIL SPIRITS.

AND TO CHEER MYSELF UP BY MAKING ME LOOK AS GLAMOROUS AS HELL.

AND THEN I KEPT A DATE WITH A FRIEND.

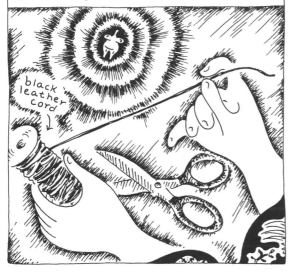

black leather cord

AND TIED HER AROUND MY NECK.

IT WAS TEN DAYS AFTER MY SURGERY. WE WERE WANDERING AROUND THE MUSEUM ACROSS THE STREET FROM THE HOSPITAL.

By then I'd lost fifteen pounds

FRIDAY AFTERNOON. I'D JUST HAD MY POST-OP CHECKUP WITH DR. CHU.

You're looking so much better!*

* Translation: It's so nice to see you when you're not TRIPPING.

BY THAT TIME, MY DRAINS HAD BEEN REMOVED AND MY INCISIONS WERE HEALING NICELY.

I just wish I could tell you the results of your tissue and lymph node analysis.

I'm hoping the lab gets back to me before the end of the day.

a. Slight mounds from pre-implant expanders

WE WERE WAITING FOR HER TO CALL JIM'S CELL IF AND WHEN THE LAB CAME THROUGH. HERE AMONG THE ROMAN GRAVE STELES.

Listen to this inscription.

I am ash. Ash is earth. Earth is a goddess. Therefore I am not dead.

Still not comfortable carrying a purse

I TURNED TO JIM.

If the results are bad. If the worst happens. I want this on my

I'll keep that in mind. But I'm quite certain we won't be planning your funeral for another forty years.

FINALLY WE GAVE UP AND DROVE BACK BEFORE RUSH HOUR, MAKING RESERVATIONS AT THE OARSMAN ALONG THE WAY.

JIM'S RINGTONE. HIS VOICE ANSWERING IT, HIS STRONG HAND OFFERING THE PHONE TO ME.

SHE'D WORKED LATE AND CHECKED FOR THE LAB REPORT ONCE MORE BEFORE SHE WENT HOME.

...And there it was! No other cancer aside from DCIS in the right breast...

...The left breast was clean and the lymph nodes we removed were clean.

You're cured!

Thank you thank you thank you thank—

JIM THANKED HER TOO AND PUT THE PHONE AWAY AND LIFTED HIS DRINK. AND THE HUMOR SEEMED TO GO OUT OF HIS EYES.

To you.

WE CLINKED, AND HIS EYES LIT UP AGAIN.

Thank God. I could never have raised those kids by myself.

CHAPTER
FOURTEEN:

Goddess Tits

THREE DAYS LATER: THE CAPE.

Coin-operated viewing machines

WHERE MY MOTHER HAD GONE TO
RECOVER FROM HER MASTECTOMY
TWENTY-ONE YEARS AGO,
WITHOUT ANY HELP FROM ME.

Fake rubber that fits in a pocket of her special suit bra

her bikini, finally a thing of the past

Still her signature bathing suit color sapphire

WHERE WE'D GONE WHEN ALICE
WAS IN HER LAST SUMMER AND
WE'D STILL WANTED TO TAKE
TEDDY TO SEE THE BEACH.

Best. To your

wondering if she'll be alive when we get back

WHERE THE ROCKS HAD TO BE SMOOTH AND ROUND AND JUST THE RIGHT SIZE BEFORE I SLIPPED THEM INTO MY BIKINI IN FARMHOUSE POND.

I'D CHECKED OUT A MASTECTOMY BRA PLACE WITH A FRIEND BACK HOME, BUT DECIDED TO SETTLE FOR A FLAT-CHESTED SUIT AT MACY'S.

my old boss martha, whose oldest kid was now in high school

I don't want to swim with a lot of crap in my bra. Look, who's to know I don't have any tits? For all they know, I'm just super fucking flat.

THE EXPANDERS WHICH HAD BEEN PLACED IN SLITS IN MY PECTORAL MUSCLES HAD YET TO BE INJECTED WITH SALINE AND WERE TINY MOUNDS.

I like being flat-chested. It's low-maintenance.

where were you when I was thirteen?

I WASN'T THINKING ABOUT HOW MY FLAT CHEST WOULD LOOK TO THOSE WHO KNEW ME.

my baby girl! Oh, sweetheart, I missed you so much. How ARE you?!

WHOA

OR HOW IT WOULD FEEL.

HE'D PICKED THE LAST TWO WEEKS TO BECOME A MAN.

TEDDY DIDN'T NEED A HUG. HE STROLLED THROUGH THE YARD AND SEEMED SURPRISED TO SEE ME.

I LOOKED AT THE DAMAGE. IT HAD HAPPENED WITHOUT ME.

305

AND THE PRESENTS I'D BROUGHT THEM WOULD NEVER MAKE UP FOR IT.

I STEADIED MYSELF. THIS WAS NOT FIXABLE. BUT WE COULD PASS THROUGH IT WITH SOME GRACE IF I LED THE WAY.

BY "EVERYBODY", SHE MEANT MY SISTER'S KIDS AND MY BROTHER'S KIDS—THE COUSINS, WHO WERE ALSO THERE FOR THE SUMMER.

MY MOTHER TOLD ME TO SWIM IN THE SEA.

I DID SWIM IN THE SEA.

AND I PERFORMED THE RECOMMENDED POST-SURGICAL STRETCHES IN THE CORNER OF OUR ROOM.

MY TORSO, I NOW REALIZED, WAS BY GIORGIO DE CHIRICO.

I WAS MY MOTHER.

I WAS MY OTHER MOTHER.

I WAS A GODDESS, JUST LIKE THEM. IT CAME WITH A KIND OF PEACE I'D NEVER FELT BEFORE.

perfect eyesight now →

AS IF ALL THE ANXIETY OVER SMALL THINGS HAD BURNED OFF ME IN THE FIRE OF REENTRY, THE FIRE OF BEING AFRAID I WAS GOING TO DIE.

AND AS I TOOK THE FIRST TENTATIVE STEPS INTO MY SECOND LIFE, I KNEW ONLY ONE THING.

I SURE AS SHIT WASN'T GOING TO SCREW THIS UP.

AT SEVEN O'CLOCK IN THE MORNING I WALKED DOWN TO THE BEACH TO GIVE MY FIRST YOGA CLASS A TRY.

the flyer in the coffee shop said to bring a towel

I COULDN'T BEGIN TO DO WHAT THEY WERE DOING DOWN THERE ON THE SAND. SO I WATCHED THEM FROM THE PARKING LOT.

THE SIGHT OF ALL THAT STRENGTH IN THE SPARKLING MORNING LIGHT... I WAS BEGINNING TO RECOGNIZE HER WORK.

AND I PROMISED MY BODY THAT IT COULD HAVE THIS. THAT IT WOULD DO THIS. THAT IT WAS GOING TO BE LOVED.

WHEN WE WENT HOME, I SIGNED UP FOR A BEGINNER YOGA CLASS AT THE GYM.

THE TEACHER WAS A LARGE AND LOVING GRANDMOTHER FROM INDIA.

AS SHE HAD BEEN TAUGHT IN INDIA, SHE TAUGHT US BREATHING, MEDITATION, AND PHILOSOPHY— NOT SIMPLY THE ASANAS.

SOME DAYS I THOUGHT SHE WAS PUTTING US ON.

BUT ALL THE OTHER DAYS MY MAT BECAME THE MOST IMPORTANT PLACE.

THE PLACE WHERE I STRETCHED AND STRENGTHENED UNTIL I COULD FINALLY DO DOWN DOG.

WHERE I SORT OF SCANNED MY BODY EACH DAY TO FEEL WHETHER ANYTHING WAS WRONG.

AND WHERE I WAS REMINDED TO THANK THE GODDESS FOR HER UNDENIABLE PRESENCE IN MY LIFE.

Hey there.

I SIGNED UP FOR SOMETHING ELSE AT THE GYM - A WORKSHOP CALLED "HEALING AS TRANSFORMATION."

I'm Ron. I'm from Amsterdam. I'm a third-generation vegetarian.

mats

cancer survivors

THE LEADER TALKED ABOUT HOW WE'D ALL BEEN GIVEN THIS ONCE-IN-A-LIFETIME OPPORTUNITY TO REVOLUTIONIZE OURSELVES.

chemo chills

So. Damn. Lucky.

the only one not currently undergoing treatment

WE WERE ALL LOOKING AT FACTORS LIKE DIET, EXERCISE, STRESS, AND ENVIRONMENTAL TOXINS TO AVOID. BUT THE WORKSHOP WENT DEEPER.

What "if" - and it's a big "if" - cancer was our body's way of telling us we were no longer truly "inhabiting" ourselves?

I know. I'm blowing your minds.

312

SOMEBODY SAID THEY DIDN'T UNDERSTAND.

The "spirit" is gone. So the "body" follows. We just don't "know" it yet.

HER AIR QUOTES AT LAST LANDED ON ME LIKE FISH HOOKS AND HER IDEA DUG NEATLY INTO MY FLESH.

So maybe the most important thing you can do to return your body to health is to "find your true path."

To remove all the blockages of your life-giving energy.

ow!

and wouldn't that be the ultimate "transformation"?

I STRUGGLED AGAINST THE SUDDENLY FAMILIAR MIX OF GUILT AND FRUSTRATION.

So you're saying, we can't help what's in our food or our environment, much less genetics, but we didn't live our lives right. So we're still to blame.

But it's a— "transformation."

I SHOOK MY HEAD.

No, it isn't. It's a punishment. If we don't find our true path, we'll get sick again and it'll be our fault.

But it's an opportunity—

I COULD FEEL A CHOICE RESONATING...

There's this thing I love in yoga where you let go of attachments.

Your attachment to the past— that's regret. Anxiety— that's an over-attachment to the future.

Let go of both and you're free.

(THIS NEXT PART, I'M PARAPHRASING.)

I don't think we're letting go of some attachments here. I'm feeling regretful and pretty goddamn anxious after listening to this.

PRESENT

hands-free

So I'm gonna follow my good feelings now. In fact, I'm gonna follow them right out this door.

WITHOUT A TWINGE OF GUILT. TRAVELING ALONE TOWARD JOY.

Jeez, what a bitch.

TRANSFORMATION. I COULDN'T GET THAT HOOK OUT OF MY SKIN.

Do you have any Daikon? I'm sorry, I don't know what that is.

vegan cookbook

vege

earthy

RAW

SUPPLEMEN

Sign This Petition!

I'D BEEN A SORT OF LOWFAT MORE-OR-LESS VEGETARIAN SINCE MY HIPPIE DAYS. NOW I GOT AN EDUCATION.

Okay. I'll have the turnips to cleanse my blood, then the brown rice for fiber, and the carrot/apple juice for vitamin C.

AND WHAT I LEARNED WAS, WE ALL HAVE OUR LIMITS.

Seriously. How can you eat that? Doesn't it taste like shit?

Yes.

BUT WE CAN ALSO SURPRISE OURSELVES.

Gave up coffee? And white sugar? Don't you miss

I miss the smell.

But not the nausea, the sweats, the headaches, and that late-afternoon crash.

THE MAIN THING WAS NOT TO WORRY ABOUT SURPRISING OTHERS.

So what do you drink, like, herbal stuff?

What am I, a pussy? Hi. I'd like a really tea.

IN THE FALL, THE PLASTIC SURGEON STARTED THE PROCESS OF RECONSTRUCTING MY BREASTS.

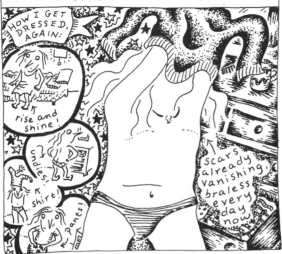

WHICH, TO BE HONEST, WAS DEFINITELY ABOUT NOT SURPRISING OTHERS.

I knew a woman in the East Village, older woman, who had an absolutely flat chest. No nipples. You could see it through her shirt.

stopped smoking

stopped drinking temporarily

She'd had a double mastectomy and she was just like, this is who I am. Deal with it.

Yeah. Wow. No.

NOW THAT I'D BEEN FLAT FOR A WHILE, I WANTED TO MAKE PEOPLE COMFORTABLE. TO ALLOW THEM TO FORGET WHAT I'D BEEN THROUGH.

And I don't want to be stuffing my bra. I don't want to wear a bra ever again.

WHICH BRINGS US TO THE NURSE WHO BROUGHT US THE BUCKET OF RUBBER BOOBS.

A SEA OF RUBBER BOOBS. ALL DIFFERENT SIZES.

So you can decide what size you'd like to be. That way the doctor knows how much to fill up your expanders.

JIM DOVE RIGHT IN, HAULING UP THE BIGGEST ONES.

What about these?

Ow, my back.

I RUMMAGED AROUND AND FOUND SOME DOUBLE-A'S.

How about these? Little fried eggs that won't hurt my back at all.

Sigh...

A PANG.

I knew it.

You miss them.

Oh come on, I was just fooling around!

317

I'D ONLY ALLOWED MYSELF TO MOURN THE LOSS ONCE SINCE MY SURGERY.

I'M gonna go take a shower.

JIM HAD ADAPTED SO DEFTLY.

Come to Papa!

Still with the octopus hands

AND WHAT I'D WRITTEN FOR MY HIGH SCHOOL ALUMNAE MAGAZINE CLASS NOTES WAS TRUE:

I wouldn't trade having my breasts back for the wisdom I have gained.

yes

BUT NOW AND THEN THE FLOOR GAVE WAY BENEATH ME AND I FOUND MYSELF FREE-FALLING INTO THIS PLACE, THIS GRIEF.

Sssshhh.

BUT IT WAS A LONG WAY DOWN, AND SO I'D LEARNED TO PULL UP, PULL UP, BACK INTO THE PRESENT.

Most women get the size they had before.

Ssshhh...

Sorry - what?

FOR A MOMENT, I'M BLANK, THINKING OF ALL THE SIZES I'VE BEEN THROUGH.

FLAT FRONT-CLASP POST-SURGICAL NUMBER

BAA

NURSING BRA VAST

38C UNDER-WIRE

THEN:

a C-cup. Yeah, I think that'll feel more normal for me.

SHE LEFT US IN AN EXAMINING ROOM, WHERE I WRAPPED MYSELF IN PAPER. ON THE TABLE: A HORSE-SIZED SYRINGE FULL OF FLUID.

Is that the saline? They're gonna stick that thing in me? Oh my God!

Better you than me.

large animal vet style

EMPTY

HE CHUCKLED.

I have an idea. Why don't we test it out on you first? You pull down your pants and I'll inject this stuff straight into your balls.

C-cups

THAT'S WHEN THE DOCTOR CAME IN.

Don't worry, you won't feel a thing. The scar tissue has very little sensation.

"Lipo for lunch"

Botox, Baby!!

I ONLY FELT PRESSURE ON THE MUSCLES OF MY CHEST AS THE SALINE PUFFED UP THE EXPANDERS, BUT HE WAS RIGHT. NO PAIN.

Shouldn't take too many visits to get these where you want them.

We left enough skin so it won't need much time to stretch.

BETWEEN SIX MONTHS AND A YEAR AFTER THE EXPANDERS SETTLED, HE'D GIVE ME MY NEW BOOBS.

It's a short outpatient procedure. Two little incisions near the armpits.

Pull out the expanders, slide in the implants.

THEN-NIPPLE RECONSTRUCTION.

OR... I GET A COUPLE OF MACHINE GUN NIPPLES THAT I CAN FIRE AT WILL LIKE THE CHICKS IN AUSTIN POWERS.

OR... FORGET THE NIPPLES. LEAVE THE SALINE SISTERS SMOOTH AND TATTOO THEM WITH A PAIR OF BADASS DRAGONS.

BUT NO MORE CUTTING INTO MY SKIN.

ALL I WANTED WERE A COUPLE OF PLAUSIBLE BUMPS UNDER MY SHIRT THAT WOULD LET MY LIFE GO BACK TO NORMAL.

SPIDERS HAD TAKEN OVER MY STUDIO. I SWEPT THEM OUT AND STARTED PAINTING WHERE I'D LEFT OFF.

AND I THOUGHT ABOUT COMICS.

DEVOURING THEM ON MY LUNCH HOUR.

BUT IT WAS LIKE CHEATING ON MY HUSBAND, THE THOUGHT OF ACTUALLY MAKING THEM.

SO I JUST LET THE DESIRE BUILD. WONDERING IF THIS WAS THE TRANSFORMATION.

THE THERAPIST I'D TALKED TO BEFORE MY SURGERY HAD WANTED TO SEE HOW I WAS DOING AFTERWARD. I WENT TO HER ONE LAST TIME.

SHE ASKED ME HOW I WAS DOING.

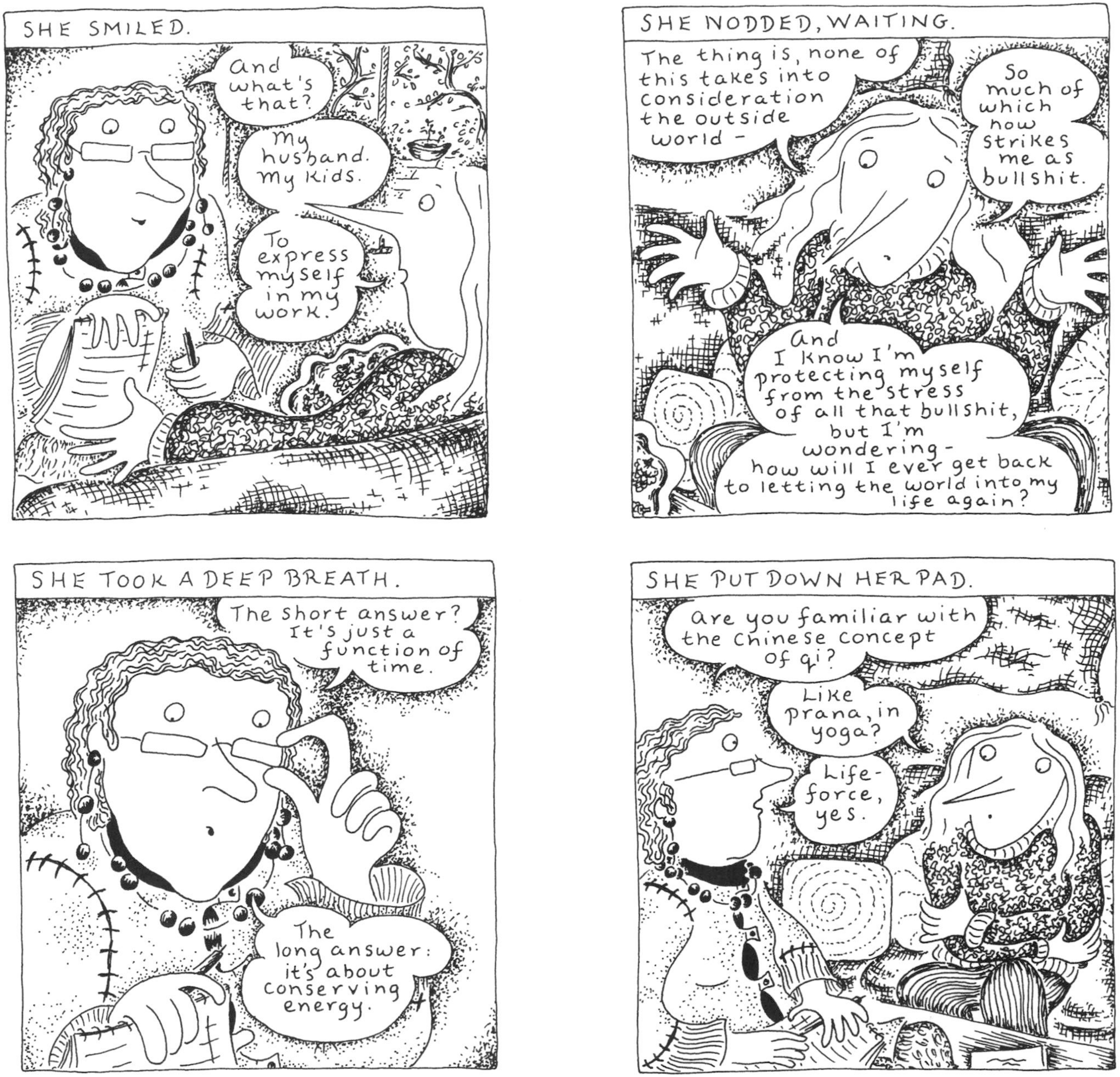
SHE SMILED.
And what's that?
My husband. My kids.
To express myself in my work.
SHE NODDED, WAITING.
The thing is, none of this takes into consideration the outside world -
So much of which now strikes me as bullshit.
And I know I'm protecting myself from the stress of all that bullshit, but I'm wondering - how will I ever get back to letting the world into my life again?
SHE TOOK A DEEP BREATH.
The short answer? It's just a function of time.
The long answer: it's about conserving energy.
SHE PUT DOWN HER PAD.
Are you familiar with the Chinese concept of qi?
Like prana, in yoga?
Life-force, yes.

HER WORDS WERE CAREFUL AND MEASURED.

I've been working with something called qigong.

The idea is to cultivate energy centers within your body and balance your qi as it flows through you.

I believe it also needs to be balanced as it flows from us and into others.

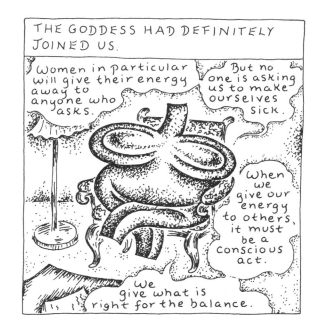

THE GODDESS HAD DEFINITELY JOINED US.

Women in particular will give their energy away to anyone who asks.

But no one is asking us to make ourselves sick.

When we give our energy to others, it must be a conscious act.

We give what is right for the balance.

A YEAR EARLIER, CIVIC GUILT AND A NEIGHBOR'S COERCION HAD CAUSED ME TO BECOME SECRETARY OF THE TOWN'S COMMUNITY GROUP.

I am writing this final item in the meeting minutes—

that I will be stepping down.

THE MONTHLY MEETINGS WERE DETAILED, ENDLESS, PRACTICAL DISCUSSIONS ABOUT THE KIND OF SHIT I'D SPENT MY LIFE AVOIDING.

What's your opinion?

I'm so sorry. I really don't have one.

325

THE BOREDOM. THE EXHAUSTION. THE HORROR.

WHAT A RELIEF FINALLY TO ADMIT THAT VOLUNTEERING WAS ABSOLUTELY NOT ONE OF THE THINGS I WAS PUT ON THIS EARTH TO DO.

In light of my recent surgery, I will be focusing on friends, family, and finding out whatever the fuck I **WAS** put on this earth to do.*

*I didn't really write that.

ON COLUMBUS DAY WEEKEND, WE DROVE UP TO DAD'S.

new front porch ↓

THE MOUNTAINS WERE COVERED WITH COLOR, AND I SAW EVERY LEAF.

ONE EVENING, HOME AGAIN, JIM AND I WENT OUT TO DINNER IN A TOWN ALONG THE DELAWARE RIVER. AFTERWARDS, WE WALKED ACROSS.

THERE WAS A GALLERY WITH LOCAL DECORATIVE ARTISTS' WORK ON THE OTHER SIDE.

I'd like to see that silver ring.

Jim waited outside

THE SURFACE BRISTLED WITH GRANULATED METAL, LIKE NO OTHER RING I'D SEEN BEFORE. I SLIPPED IT ON.

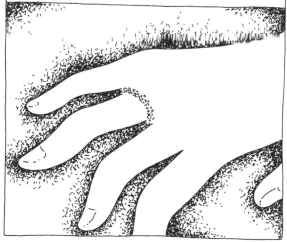

I'D BEEN DRINKING. WE'D BEEN EATING ITALIAN FOOD. I WAS ALLOWING THE WORLD IN THAT NIGHT AND I DIDN'T WANT TO FORGET.

327

THIS RING WOULD BE MY REMINDER.

To take care of you and protect you. To love and respect you. All the days of my life.

AND THAT'S HOW I MARRIED MYSELF.

What a beautiful couple. Sniff!

ONE CRISP, BRILLIANT SATURDAY TOWARD THE END OF OCTOBER, I REGISTERED FOR THE LOCAL BREAST CANCER FUNDRAISING 5K.

Are you a survivor?

Uh-yes.

Then you get a special bib. And a water bottle. And a ticket for one free donut after the run.

I DON'T RUN. I WALK. LUCKILY, THERE WAS A WALK AFTER THE RUN. I STROLLED DOWN TO THE STARTING LINE, CARRYING MY SWAG.

START HER

Pink

Pink →

I'D BEEN HESITANT ABOUT COMING TO SUCH A COMMERCIALIZED EVENT. I STILL WAS. UNTIL THE OCEAN OF WOMEN BEGAN TO MOVE.

SHOULDER TO SHOULDER, THERE WERE THOUSANDS. ON THEIR BACKS THEY CARRIED MESSAGES FOR THE WOMEN THEY'D LOST.

BACK WHEN THE NURSE HAD BEEN TAKING AWAY THE BUCKET OF BOOBS, I'D TRIED TO LOOK ON THE BRIGHT SIDE OF MY SITUATION.

SHE LOOKED AT ME WITH UTTER HUMORLESSNESS. SADNESS. REALNESS.

IT ENGULFED ME: THE SORROW AND THE STRENGTH OF THIS WAVE OF WOMEN, EVERY ONE OF US AFFECTED BY THIS DISEASE.

501
SURV

BABY FOOD!

GO IN PEACE!

DADDY TOYS!

330

I GAVE DEEP THANKS THAT SEASON FOR THANKSGIVING, CHRISTMAS AND NEW YEAR'S.

AROUND ONE P.M. NEW YEAR'S DAY, I DEVELOPED A NASTY CRAMP.

BY MIDNIGHT IT FELT LIKE A MODEST FIRE HAD BROKEN OUT UNDER MY RIGHT RIB CAGE.

DAWN, AND I'M STILL WATCHING EPISODES OF THE MUNSTERS, THE SOUNDTRACK DROWNED OUT BY THE SCREAMING PAIN INSIDE MY HEAD.

FINALLY ADMITTING IT WASN'T RUN-OF-THE-MILL INDIGESTION, I WENT TO SEE MY DOCTOR THE NEXT DAY.

SHE ORDERED AN ULTRASOUND TO FIND OUT WHAT WAS GOING ON IN THERE.

THERE WERE ABOUT A HUNDRED STONES IN MY GALLBLADDER AND FIVE BLOCKING THE DUCT.

332

HE WAS RIGHT AND I WAS INFURIATED.

THAT DID NOTHING TO PREVENT MY RAGE FROM RUMBLING TO THE SURFACE LIKE A VOLCANO.

THE VOLCANO TORE THROUGH ALL THE LAYERS OF MY RECENT PEACE AND HEALING. TORE THEM RIGHT THE FUCK OFF.

BUT NOBODY ANSWERED MY QUESTION. SO I PRESSED MY FACE TO THE TEMPLE FLOOR INSTEAD.

AND THEN, MAD LAUGHTER, AS I REALIZED I MEANT NOTHING; IT WAS ONLY A GAME: I WAS A CHEW TOY IN THE JAWS OF LIFE.

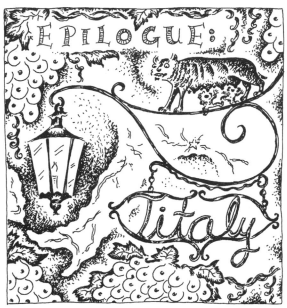

EPILOGUE: Italy

JUNE. JIM AND I STOOD IN VENICE WHILE MY BROTHER TOOK OUR PICTURE.

ON THE GRAND CANAL, OUTSIDE THE TRAIN STATION, WITH THE GREEN-DOMED CHURCH OF SAN SIMEONE PICCOLO BEHIND US.

MY WHOLE FAMILY HAD COME TO CELEBRATE MY SISTER'S FIFTIETH BIRTHDAY AT HER NEW APARTMENT IN A NEIGHBORING TOWN.

THIS MORNING WE'D ALL GOTTEN ON THE TRAIN AND SPENT THE DAY WANDERING AROUND THIS FLOATING CITY.

NOW IT WAS AFTERNOON. AND I'D DONE IT. I'D FULFILLED A LIFELONG WISH TO SEE VENICE BEFORE I DIED.

NOT THAT I WAS GOING TO CORK OFF ANYTIME SOON. I'D PASSED MY SIX-MONTH CHECKUP WITH FLYING COLORS.

IT WAS JUST THAT I FINALLY UNDERSTOOD THERE WAS NO TIME TO WASTE, EVEN IF I LIVED FOR A LONG, LONG TIME.

NOT YET I WASN'T, BUT I WAS CLOSE. THE GRAPHIC NOVEL I WANTED TO MAKE WAS READY, IN MY HEAD. BUT NOW... THE FEAR.

NO.

FIVE MONTHS LATER I'D LET GO OF THAT LEDGE AND LEARN THE ART OF SAILING THROUGH THE AIR.

BY WHICH I MEAN, SAT MY ASS DOWN AND BEGAN DRAWING AND WRITING THE PICTURES THAT TOLD MY STORY.

THAT SAME NOVEMBER I COMPLETED THE BREAST RECONSTRUCTION PROCESS, RECEIVING MY PERMANENT IMPLANTS.

They look a little square, but whatever.

What did you think you were going to look like, a Playboy centerfold?

guitar porn

I HAD NOT OPTED, IN THE END, FOR TATTOOS OR MACHINE GUNS. THE SALINE SISTERS WERE AS SMOOTH AS SPACE ORBS.

No. But the thing is... Kids ruined my waist, veins ruined my legs, and now my chest has been maimed.

Guitar Wanker magazines

also a little uneven

And I'm not ready to give up my sex appeal yet. But I'm trying to figure out where it's going to come from.

JIM COCKED HIS HEAD.

Don't you know guys like personality?

OH MY GOD. SO I WAS BACK THERE AGAIN.

No, I mean it. Some women are all built and everything, and the vibe they give off isn't sexy at all.

Panel 1: I CROSSED MY ARMS AND WAITED.

Other women just have that woomf. It's not about what kind of a rack they have.

They've got that vibe. Deep down. That's what I find sexy.

Panel 2: LYING BASTARD.

Panel 3: THE WOMEN HERE WERE ALL SO GENETICALLY GIFTED AND WELL-PACKAGED THAT MY HUSBAND AND MY BROTHER HAD RENAMED THE PLACE:

Titaly.

Absolutely.

Panel 4: AND I WAS ENVIOUS, OF COURSE, BUT I'D ALSO BEGUN TO GET USED TO THE IDEA THAT MY TITS WERE NEVER ACTUALLY ME.

I'm still here, even if my tits aren't. I'm still a woman. I'm still me. Tits. I always thought they were so important. But this is who I really am.

Honey, you're preaching to the choir.

TOWARD THE END OF THE SUMMER, RIGHT BEFORE THE ANNIVERSARY OF MY SURGERY, I'D BE FEELING SORRY FOR MYSELF AGAIN.

Want a cigarette?

No thanks, I quit.

WHY WAS I THE ONLY ONE WHO COULDN'T JUST ENJOY THIS, WHO WAS ALWAYS WAITING FOR THE OTHER SHOE TO DROP?

I think I'll smoke this later.

IT WAS LIKE A SCAB I COULD NEVER STOP PICKING.

wondering if I'll get cancer again; and if so, where; and when? I mean, exactly how much time do I have? And how come if just worrying about it will make me get it?

Jesus, girl. you gotta get off this ride.

WITHIN SIX MONTHS, I SEEMED TO BE THE LUCKY ONE.

husband would commit suicide

would get a divorce, breast cancer diagnosis, and mastectomy

341

AND SO I'D LEARN TO SHAKE IT OFF, REALIZING THAT EVERYONE GETS THEIR TURN. ALL YOU CAN DO IS CELEBRATE MAKING IT THROUGH.

Mom, what's this?

SO LONG! GO IN PEACE DADDY TOYS EMBRACE THE GODDESS!

I'd just found it in my portfolio

AND GIVE THE DAMAGE ITS DUE.

It's a picture I made before my surgery.

Are those your boobs?

BECAUSE NOW IT'S A MEMBER OF THE FAMILY.

Yes, honey.

I miss them.

Oh, me too.

JEN BECAME IN MANY WAYS OLD BEFORE HER TIME.

I'm so sorry, Sweetie. I shouldn't have left this out. I was about to put it away.

No, I like it, mom.

GODDESS!

Can I have it in my room?

TEDDY SHARED LESS OF HIS FEELINGS WITH ME; HE BECAME CLOSER TO HIS FATHER.

I CALLED THE SOCIAL WORKER LISTED IN THE SUPPORT MATERIAL FROM THE HOSPITAL AND ASKED HER IF I SHOULD TAKE THE KIDS TO THERAPY.

From what you've said, it doesn't sound like their reactions are outside the range of normal.

Are you sure?

In general, with small children, taking them to therapy sends a strong signal that something's wrong.

I don't advise it unless the behavior's acute.

SO I DECIDED TO LET THEM HEAL THEMSELVES.

I ALSO TOOK MY ONCOLOGIST'S ADVICE AND GOT TESTED FOR THE BRCA GENE MUTATION ASSOCIATED WITH INHERITED BREAST AND OVARIAN CANCERS.

It's negative. You do not have the genetic mutation.

testing counselor

EVEN ALLOWING FOR AN ELEVEN PERCENT CHANCE OF TEST ERROR, I STILL COULDN'T BELIEVE IT.

So even though my mother and I had the same cancer in the same breast, it wasn't genetic?

That's right. But you could both share other factors that predispose you for this type of cancer... We just don't know what those factors are.

SO WE GO ON, LIVING WITH OUR UNCERTAINTIES.

JIM WOULDN'T LET ME TAKE THE TIE OFF THE TOWEL RACK. IT'S STILL THERE, NINE YEARS LATER.

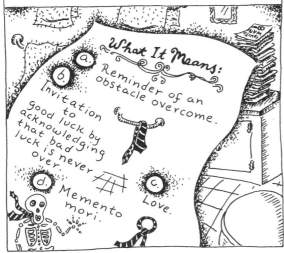

What It Means:

a. Reminder of an obstacle overcome.

b. Invitation to good luck by acknowledging that bad luck is never over.

c. Love.

d. Memento mori.

THE HOT AND ANCIENT WIND SNAPPED MY HAIR LIKE A WHIP.

a bunch of them, actually...

I said: kiss me.

344

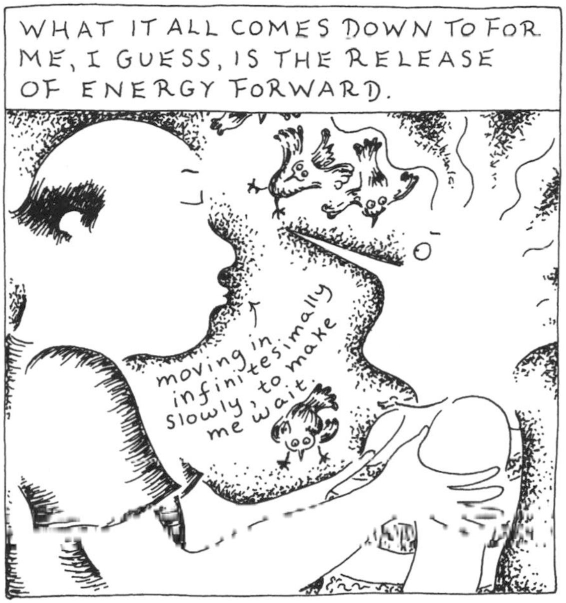
WHAT IT ALL COMES DOWN TO FOR ME, I GUESS, IS THE RELEASE OF ENERGY FORWARD.
moving infinitesimally slowly, to make me wait.

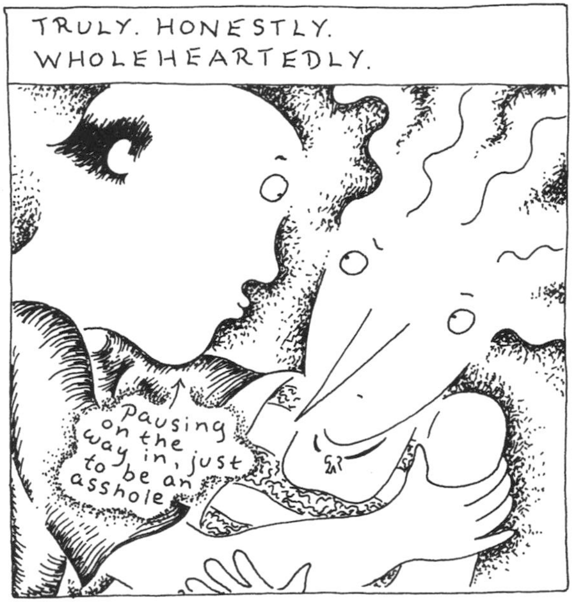
TRULY. HONESTLY. WHOLEHEARTEDLY.
pausing on the way in, just to be an asshole

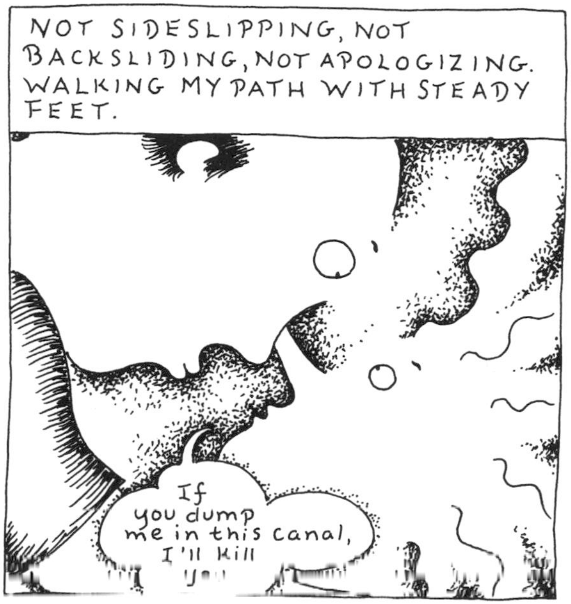
NOT SIDESLIPPING, NOT BACKSLIDING, NOT APOLOGIZING. WALKING MY PATH WITH STEADY FEET.
If you dump me in this canal, I'll kill

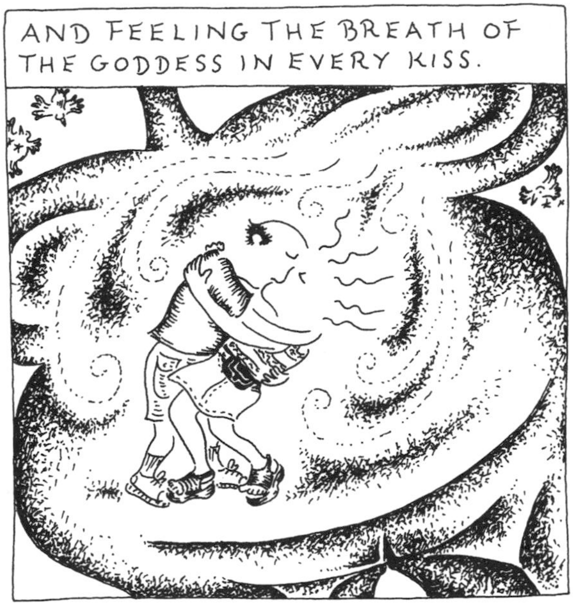
AND FEELING THE BREATH OF THE GODDESS IN EVERY KISS.

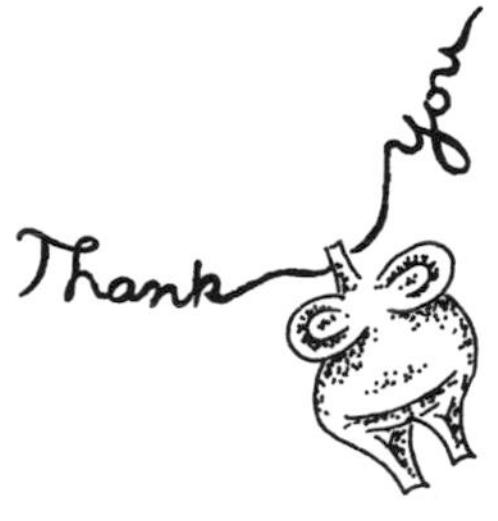
Thank you

Acknowledgments:

Without you this eight-year project would never have reached the last page: Mom and Dad, who somewhere along the way made the stupid, brave choice to let me do my thing; Marisa Marchetto, whose first Cancer Vixen comic helped inspire this book; Chris Staros, patient prince of comix publishing; Dean Haspiel, who once opened the door to me in Gowanus, Brooklyn and has mentored me ever since; Nica Lalli, who always seemed to be the older one even though she was the younger one and knew just what to do; Rick Parker, who offered support and guidance and sent me a dip pen when my rapidograph gave me tendonitis two years before this book was finished; Glynnis Fawkes, comix artist, mom and partner in crime; Marina, Elizabeth, and Gale, sister goddesses forever; Emma O'Connor, who scanned and photo-shopped two summers' worth of this book; Helen Law, whose miraculous acupuncture keeps me able to do what I do; and my whole family, whose stories I have stolen with love and sympathy and joy that this is life. I am so glad to have shared it with you.

mwah!